ONLY THE BEST IS GOOD ENOUGH

THE STORY OF CAMPERDOWN HIGH SCHOOL

BASIL K. BRYAN

The Story of Camperdown High School
All Rights Reserved.
Copyright © 2022 Basil K. Bryan
v4.0, r1.1

The opinions expressed in this manuscript are solely the opinions of the author and do not represent the opinions or thoughts of the publisher. The author has represented and warranted full ownership and/or legal right to publish all the materials in this book.

This book may not be reproduced, transmitted, or stored in whole or in part by any means, including graphic, electronic, or mechanical without the express written consent of the publisher except in the case of brief quotations embodied in critical articles and reviews.

Outskirts Press, Inc.
http://www.outskirtspress.com

Paperback ISBN: 978-1-9772-4897-8
Hardback ISBN: 978-1-9772-5016-2

Cover Photo © 2022 Basil K. Bryan. All rights reserved - used with permission.

Outskirts Press and the "OP" logo are trademarks belonging to Outskirts Press, Inc.

PRINTED IN THE UNITED STATES OF AMERICA

To the memory of Jean Marie Pinnock Bryan

She was all Camperdown:

- Kindergarten School
- Preparatory School
- High School
- Form Captain
- House Captain
- Games Captain
- School Prefect
- Head Girl
- Valedictorian

A highly respected administrator at Howard University in Washington, D.C., Jean Bryan served as Director of the University's Educational Advisory Center in the College of Arts and Sciences. She impacted thousands of lives and inspired her students with the African Proverb: "Tomorrow belongs to those who plan for it today."

Life is one big road, with lots of signs,
So when you riding through the ruts,
don't complicate your mind;
Flee from hate, mischief and jealousy.
Don't bury your thoughts, put your vision to reality.

(Bob Marley)

Hold fast to dreams
For if dreams die
Life is a broken-winged bird
That cannot fly

(Langston Hughes)

Contents

Author's Note i
Founder and Principal vii
Camperdown Principals Over the Years ix
Mission, Vision, Core Values xi
Quick Facts xiii

Chapter 1:   Ivy May Wilson Grant—A Life of Purpose 1
Chapter 2:   Going by Faith, Making a Way: 1930s – 1950s ... 12
               A Pictorial Journey (1930s – 1950s) 32
Chapter 3:   Major Building Years: 1960s – 1970s 40
Chapter 4:   Solum Optima: *To Seek the Best* 84
Chapter 5:   Forward Camperdown: The Journey Continues 106
               Pictorial Journey (1960s forward) 129

Appendix 1:   School Prospectus – Year 1947 163
Appendix 2:   Camperdown Student Term Report 177
Appendix 3:   Camperdown School Leaving Certificate 179
Appendix 4:   School Song—"Foundation" 181
Appendix 5:   Graduation Song—"Leaving School" 183
Appendix 6:   Camperdown at the Penn Relays 185

Appendix 7:	Nation Movers (Footballers) (Olympians)	187
Appendix 8:	C'Down 100: Changemakers	190
Sources		199
Index		200

Author's Note

Camperdown High School, seen by many as "The Diamond in the East," has garnered unparalleled accomplishments in multiple areas, not the least of which are in sports and academics. Situated in East Kingston, Jamaica, the school is historically referred to as "The Sprint Factory," a name that fittingly highlights the extraordinary athletic success of the institution, particularly in the sport of track and field. As phenomenal as that success is, the Sprint Factory, however, tells the story of a Cinderella-like beginning that has morphed into a multi-complex institution, producing well-rounded students who excel at the scholastic level and in the wider society.

Driven by a *modus operandi* that highlights sacrifice, determination, success despite the odds, and resilience, all nicely captured in its motto, **Solum Optima Petenda Sunt**, students are expected to "be the best you can be," "be all you can be," "be a top student," "be a volunteer;" cajoled to "be involved in community service," "be part of the solution," and expected to "be a leader, never forgetting that the essence of leadership is humility in service."

After twenty years as student, teacher and administrator, Valentine Bailey was appointed in 2010 as Principal of Camperdown. His was not a "love-at-first-sight" affair. Bailey mentions that in 1977, "I watched as my friends celebrated, they had passed their Common Entrance [Examination] and were on their way to Jamaica College. I was happy for them," he remembers, "but sad for me, I had 'failed.'"

His teacher tried to console him: "You are too young and so they want you to try again next year."

"The following year I picked for Camperdown High," he continues, "no more Wolmer's or JC [Jamaica College]; furthermore, my brother had been attending Camperdown and he had only good things to say about the school, so I said, why not!...I have witnessed first-hand how Mrs. Grant's dream has become a reality for so many, helping to shape so many lives."

Camperdown's history in drawing out the best from its students is cemented into a design that prioritizes academic competence, yet placing added focus on co-curricular accomplishments. The school's achievements in so many different areas have produced the Camperdown of today, that "Diamond in the East."

Camperdown is home to almost two thousand students, a far cry from the 300 students the "new" Camperdown opened with in 1958, and a monumental achievement over the four little girls who started back in 1930. Indeed, Camperdown has expanded into a giant oasis. Collectively, a sense of family and bonding is nurtured; an atmosphere of togetherness conjured. It is this bond of family, driven by stellar achievements, that motivates the students to excel and, when they do, celebrate as lustily as they can.

The birth of Camperdown coincided with the nationalistic awakenings of the 1920s and 1930s and the urgent need for educational opportunities to that vast section of the country's student population that was badly neglected, even ignored.

Thus came Camperdown!

Some of the schools that came out of this realization were good; some were not. Many fell by the wayside. Camperdown was among those that thrived.

Among the several societal challenges that Camperdown sought to address was how to satisfy the unquenchable desire of the ordinary people to see positive and lasting changes in their lives.

In the words of the founder, Mrs. Ivy May Wilson Grant, spoken in 1968: "The vibrant, vigorous Camperdown you see today is the substance of a dream which took its form and shape in the last decades. From its inception, Camperdown was sought after and came into being to satisfy a need. Parents considered the development of their children's **character as basic a need as physical and mental growth**, and for this reason Camperdown was sought out, was preferred, and was chosen. "

Putting together this story was no easy task – non-existent files, missing records, faded memories. And as with any telling and retelling of a story, omissions will occur and some things might seem to carry a different meaning based on who is the story-teller. Yet it seemed to me that it was vastly necessary to undertake this project. After all, from such an inauspicious start, Camperdown has given to the nation Olympic medalists, artistes, musicians, public servants and political leaders of national and international fame, men and women in various disciplines and professions, who shrugged off their humble beginnings to rise to the highest levels in their respective endeavours. I thought this was a story that deserved to be told.

What followed came about in an almost accidental way. With such a mindset, I was drawn to a statement by Mr. William Watson, then-President of the Camperdown High School Alumni Association in Jamaica. Said Watson: "Most of us [students] who attended Camperdown High graduated without an awareness or full knowledge of the institution and its founder, Ivy Grant. We intend to change that and educate the current generation of the brilliance that came out of our **alma mater**, showcasing Mrs. Grant's contribution to education and nation building."

I decided then, yes, this story was important and needed to be told, in particular to shine a light to later generations of Camperdownians (and others) who need to know and reflect on the history of an institution that has brought much joy to the society and has led to many lifelong friendships.

As one who attended the school, has given back over the years, and take particular pride in the school's many accomplishments, I settled on the task with diligence, as difficult as it seemed to me at the outset.

What I have tried to do was to come up with a faithful compilation/chronology of the development and achievements of the school over the 90 years of its existence. Though the road ahead seemed long, I decided that it was well worth the effort. It tells the story of some of the most impactful chapters in Camperdown's history. It is my trust that this book will be a reference for what has been achieved and a guide to what can be achieved if we put our minds to the tasks.

This book reflects input by a number of persons who dedicated themselves with oftentimes unbridled enthusiasm, even those who had little or no connection with the school, but nonetheless wanted to make a contribution. A few alumni – including some who attended in the 1940s and 1950s – were more than willing to dig deep into their memory banks and sought to contribute in any way they could. Many hours were spent in interviews.

As to be expected, at times memories were faded, and whatever was "remembered" had to be checked and compared, reviewed many times over, in order to ensure that the essence of the stories, at a minimum, was in alignment.

Several past students shared information—Richard Grant (son of the founder); Ms. Claudette Wilson (niece of Mrs. Grant); Mrs. Irene (Reid) Walter; Dr. Marcianne (Harriott) Harris; and Mrs. Merle (Wilson) Meeks, who spoke from their experiences as Camperdown students during the 1940s or 1950s. My task was to ask questions that would help them to dig deep into their memories and to weld together their stories. Among a later generation of past students who readily answered the call, I give thanks to the following: Jackie Lucie-Smith, Cynthia (Warren) Cooke, Glen Mills, Marcia (Smith) Moo Young, Everald Fletcher, John Wilson, Valerie (Johnson) Owen, Emmett DeCambre, Eric Barrett, Michael Brown, Andrew Hines, Eron Smith, Christopher Bender, Boris Robinson, Adrian McLean, Faith Simpson, and Cheryl Rigg.

Grace Smith (daughter of Mrs. Winifred Smith) was helpful in providing tidbits from her mother's old papers that gave insight into the Camperdown of the 1940s when her mother and aunt (Ms. Norma Crooks) both attended the school.

Among the teachers who were helpful with information are Mr. Dennis Webster, Dean of Discipline at the school and later Acting Vice-Principal; Mrs. Janise Campbell-Lee (Head of Physical Education and Sports Coordinator); and Mrs. Judith Stampp (School Librarian), who engagingly "discovered" some vintage photographs.

I am grateful to Ms. Krystle Jones, who readily offered her help in researching and editing. Dr. Elka Wiley Mills offered help with editing and made valuable suggestions. Mr. Joe King spent much time meticulously going through multiple edits, and did the seemingly impossible – "resurrecting" many of the time-worn images – all in an effort to give a more enhanced photographic substance to the story. Even without saying so, he merely wanted to ensure that the final product would reflect the ideal of the school's motto, that is, to seek and present the best. To him heartfelt gratitude! Thanks also to Senator Paul Miller, a former member of the Jamaican Senate. Through him I was able to gain access to the store of information on Camperdown reposed in the library of the United Church of Jamaica. Ms. Sheree Rhoden of the Gleaner library was very cooperative in helping to source Camperdown's history. Mr. Junior Lincoln (in Jamaica), Mrs. Merline Barton, Mrs. Sandra Pinnock Wiley, Mrs. Kimetha Knowles, and Mrs. Marchelle Wiley Smith (in Florida), were reliable and constant sources of encouragement and support throughout the various stages of researching and writing.

I must also extend my gratitude to the Honourable Dr. Vincent HoSang and his Family Foundation and to the Honourable Earl Jarrett and the Jamaica National Group for their kind assistance.

To them all, thanks for the support; thanks for the inspiration; thanks for the love!

The story of Camperdown High School and its founder, Ivy Grant, is replicated every day in Jamaica. Much like Camperdown, there are nuggets to be found throughout the communities all over our blessed country, Jamaica. Yes, even in the underserved communities that oftentimes we neglect at our peril.

It is my hope that those who have benefited from the Camperdown experience will remain proud of their **alma mater**. They, too, must join in sharing the story. After all, it is up to us – the beneficiaries of that dream – to realize that each generation must sing its own song and write its own history. But it is incumbent upon succeeding generations to also know that history and the songs of those who toiled in yesteryears to prepare the way for the coming generations. It goes without saying that in order to sing the songs of the past generations, we must know the words of the songs and the meaning of those words.

Despite the enduring challenges of limited resources, Camperdown continues to be inspired by its Latin motto: **Solum Optima Petenda Sunt**

– "Only the Best is Good Enough" – translated as "to seek the best," as excellence, and manifested through scholarship and sports and service, in fields of spirited competition, and in just plain, everyday humanity and service to mankind, by nurturing girls and boys into women and men of outstanding character, citizenship and work, and living out that Biblical message that redounds throughout the generations:

Inasmuch as you do it unto the least of my brothers and sisters, you do it unto me.

(Matthew 25:40)

Finally, I am thankful for the life of Jean Marie, my wife, companion, and friend of over five decades. Much of the details, observations, and reminiscences in this book first found an opening in our discussions over the many years together, and it was always a given that (if anyone should) it would fall to me to record the rich and inspiring story of Camperdown. It saddens me that she did not live to see the recorded story in full bloom. From kindergarten to preparatory to high, Camperdown was her only school. She was, after all, all Camperdown!

Founder and Principal

Ivy May Wilson Grant
1930 – 1958; 1961 – 1968

Camperdown Principals Over the Years

Noel White
1958 – 1960 (Acting)

James Fitz-Henry "Jeff"
Brown
1968 – 1982

Winifred Smith
1983 – 1992
(1982 – 1983, Acting)

Mrs. Myrtle Kellier acted as Principal 1992-93

Cynthia Cooke
1993 – 2010

Valentine Bailey
2010 –

Mission, Vision, Core Values

MISSION

The mission of Camperdown High School is to provide students with the requisite skills and attributes so that they may raise their performance and realize their full potential in an environment that delivers a prescribed curriculum, promotes learning, discipline and school-community relationships, and in which professional and quality service is provided by staff, thereby facilitating the total development of each individual and contributing to the school community and to nation-building.

VISION

With:
A caring and committed school community
Unity among stakeholders
A high quality curriculum delivery system
And students performing community service

We will produce:
The most disciplined school
Consistently high academic, vocational and extra-
Curricular achievement

And:
Well-rounded students (graduates)
Who will make an
Invaluable contribution to all aspects of society

CORE VALUES

Excellence
Discipline
Respect
Loyalty
Spirituality
Cooperation

Quick Facts

IVY MAY GRANT, O.D., M.A., B.A.

Born	February 11, 1906
1928-1929	Headmistress—North Street Seventh-day Adventist School
1930	Opens "The Home School" on her father's veranda (9 Camperdown Road)
	Moves to nearby Portland Road (#16, 16A – family-owned) shortly after
	(Kindergarten and Preparatory)
1934	Camperdown Girl School (16A Portland Road) (Kindergarten and Preparatory for Girls & Boys) (High School for girls only)
1939	Marries Norman Ernest Grant
1945	Camperdown High School (new building #16-1/2 Portland Road) (Preparatory Department for Girls and Boys) (High School for girls only)

1958	Camperdown High School becomes Grant-Aided (Co-educational)
1960	B.A.—University of London
1968	Retires after 38 years as Headmistress of Camperdown
1974	M.A.—City University of New York
1976	Order of Distinction—National Honour by the Government of Jamaica "for Service in the field of Education'"
1982	Dies October 26

Children
Richard Ernest Wilson Grant, Born January 15, 1942
Norman Ernest John Coleridge Grant, Born September 6, 1946
Paul Adrian Graham Grant, Adopted 1965

A master of the English Language, fluent in Latin, Ivy Grant epitomized EXCELLENCE

1

Ivy May Wilson Grant—A Life of Purpose

SOLUM OPTIMA PETENDA SUNT (Only the best is good enough) – has been the compass that guided the life of Ivy May Wilson Grant.

Many believe that Ivy Wilson was destined to have her own school. Family lore informs that even as a young girl she would constantly line up her three dolls as if they were young charges and, throughout the day, would teach them, reprimand them, and instruct them, in the manner of a strict disciplinarian, setting the rules to be obeyed, and exhorting them to become proper young ladies.

Ivy May Wilson was born in Saint Catherine, Jamaica on February 11, 1906. Her maternal grandfather, James Egerton Wilson, Snr., was an engineer in charge of the Bog Walk Hydro-power Plant; his wife, Catherine Wilson (Miss Katy), was a housewife. At an early age, young Ivy was adopted by her grandfather and his wife. While still a young girl, the family moved to Kingston, settling in the newly-emergent middle-class community of Rollington Town. After infant school and some private tutoring, young Ivy attended the Rollington Town Primary School. After primary school it was next to the privately-owned Clarke's School. Coming from a strong Seventh-day Adventist family, as very much expected, she was then sent to do secondary schooling at the West Indies Training College high school in Mandeville. In 1921, she was successful in the University of Cambridge Overseas Examination in Religious Knowledge, English – Grammar, Composition, and Authors, History, Geography, Algebra, and Freehand Drawing.

At the West Indies Training College (now Northern Caribbean

THE STORY OF CAMPERDOWN HIGH SCHOOL

University), she excelled, even while honing her skills in education management. After graduating there, she returned to her parents' home in Kingston and engaged in further private tutoring to prepare for the Local 1st Year examination. Thereafter, she accepted a job at a local elementary school, staying in this positon for a short time. She was later offered the job of Assistant Principal at the newly-formed Seventh-day Adventist School on North Street. Within a short time, she was appointed to the post of Principal. As Principal she sought to elevate the school, lifting the students to new heights of awareness, while believing that her young charges could become the best in the world. To this end, she introduced her students to several new initiatives, among which was the introduction of a "Fan Dance," in which the young students would do a choreographed dance routine using the fans as a tool to enhance the performance.

But lo and behold, this new maneuver, though popular with the students, drew the ire of the Adventist hierarchy and subsequently she was terminated from the job after a mere one year. Not to be down-hearted, she decided to use the time to further her studies by private tutoring in preparation of starting her own school and pursuing the London Inter-B.A. programme. The story is told by family friends that she was not satisfied with the existing education system which excluded many brilliant minds, and others who were not being challenged at the schools that were available to them.

It was during this period that she, Miss Wilson to her community, was persuaded to tutor some young children of family friends. During this period, things gathered momentum, and although it is difficult to fully comprehend the next moves, in early February of 1930, she welcomed one, two, three, and then a fourth child for tutoring. They were entrusted to her care for special private tutoring to prepare them to sit the then popular Common Entrance Examination offered to children between the age of nine to eleven to gain entry into the main high schools. Thus came CAMPERDOWN! And, according to the Professor Oscar Harriott, a long-standing family friend and classmate at the West Indies Training College, who later became a respected member of Camperdown's faculty, "she made a brilliant success of her newly formed school."

The seed of her school started on the verandah of her (adopted) father's home on Camperdown Road (by Lincoln Road) with those four students. With a new-found vigor and a fierce determination to match, Miss Wilson started building her little school with the four students. Much in line with the ethos of the times, the school was referred to as the "Home School." During that period in the country's history it was quite common to see advertisements for many "home schools" teaching basic subjects, some teaching music or art, or even personal upliftment.

The idea of helping to prepare young students to better themselves through education was much in alignment with Miss Wilson's Christian upbringing. After all, young Miss Wilson was deeply involved in church life. At the "United Sabbath Day Adventist Church" on Wildman Street, she played important roles as a Sabbath School teacher, organized and participated in Sabbath Evening Prayers (Vespers), and, being gifted with what was described as "a splendid voice," regularly performed as a soloist at many church functions. But not only was young Miss Wilson engaged in church work, she was also deeply involved in the debating and literary societies of the day, where she was not only exposed to the finer offerings in life, but also got the opportunity to meet some of the most important people in the emergent Black and Brown middle class.

Ivy Wilson would recall a speech given in 1930 on the importance of education that left an indelible impression on her as she charted the course for her school. At a private school function at which she was in attendance, the speaker emphasized that "every child should receive a good education at school for there they learnt discipline and unselfishness in dealing with other people. It was important," the speaker continued, "for everyone to have a sound education, for an uneducated man or woman was really a hopeless specimen of humanity."

Amazingly, Miss Wilson's home school grew by leaps and bounds, augmented by children of family and friends, including nieces Fay and Claudette Wilson. So impressive was the "look" of those neat little children in uniform, and so impressed was the community, that words quickly spread and after a few months the enrollment reached 42, with the stated purpose to educate girls and boys to become mature Christian citizens, and to achieve academic excellence and physical, social and spiritual maturity.

Expansion

The Home School, as Miss Wilson's school was politely called, quickly outgrew the veranda. The school was then moved to family-owned premises at 16 and 16A Portland Road shortly thereafter. *"ONLY THE BEST IS GOOD ENOUGH"* was Ivy Wilson's personal motto; it also became the school's motto. Embedded in this was the Christian belief that one should set for herself the highest goals and to make a determined effort to reach them.

A Christian, forward-thinking woman, Ivy Wilson carefully recruited a team of knowledgeable and dedicated like-minded teachers who together molded and shaped the lives of hundreds of young students who were entrusted to their care in the ensuing years. Students who attended Camperdown in the forties and fifties remember the love and care of pioneering teachers as Mrs. Myrtle Burke, Mrs. Isobel MacPherson, Mrs. Alda McCatty, Miss Girvan, Mrs. Aiken, Mrs. Nora Malcolm, Miss Rita Escoffery and Mrs. Viola Aitcheson. At Portland Road, Camperdown became a preparatory school for boys and girls. In 1934 a high school department was opened, but for girls only.

In 1939, Ivy May Wilson got married to Norman Ernest Grant, a civil servant with the Government of Jamaica. They lived at 10 Portland Road, moving to 17 Second Avenue in Mountain View Gardens, eventually settling in the family residence at 36 Sandhurst Crescent, near King's House in St. Andrew.

In 1942, son Richard Ernest Wilson Grant was born, followed by Norman Ernest John Coleridge Grant (Johnny) in 1946. The story is told that students at the school celebrated when the boys were born because on that day they got a day off from school.

The history of Camperdown cannot be told without mention of "Archdeacon," the belt used as a tool to enforce compliance and discipline among the boys. Ivy Grant's son, Richard, attended Camperdown between age three and twelve, then he left, as all boys did; he went on to attend Jamaica College. According to him, Archdeacon was a strap, one-inch-wide, and 3/8ths of an inch thick. Many who experienced it lived in fear of it. The children of mothers who were teachers at the school would be special targets – the Burkes, the Aitchesons, the Malcolms, the MacPhersons and the Grants – and had to be exemplary both in behavior and in their lessons, or else! Students who transgressed quickly had a date with Archdeacon. If they slipped up on multiplication tables, they felt it. All students were expected to know the answers to everything; the teachers' children, noticeably, were held to a much higher standard.

IVY MAY WILSON GRANT—A LIFE OF PURPOSE

The young boys, especially, would many times have an encounter with Archdeacon. One incident from the early 1940s that Richard Grant recalls, was of a group of them playing football in the school yard during break.

> The boisterous enjoyment disturbed the class, and Mrs. Aitcheson confiscated the football and locked it away in her cupboard. Unfortunately, she forgot to return it after school and left for home. David DePass, whose ball it was, decided to pick the lock on the cupboard to retrieve his ball, and fortunately, I voiced concern over his actions and left the scene of the crime. This was discovered the following day, and all who were present were hauled in front of Mrs. Grant for a taste of "Archdeacon." Fortunately for me, when it was my turn, the other boys admitted that I had cautioned them against their act and that I'd left. I was thus spared on that occasion.
>
> Mrs. Nora Malcolm was our English teacher, and although all our teachers were sticklers for all the students speaking proper English, Mrs. Malcolm reigned supreme. The story is told that one night, a thief entered her daughter Jean's bedroom and Jean, scared as hell, shouted out 'TIEF, TIEF' to which Mrs. Malcolm responded, 'Jean, the word is THIEF, NOT TIEF, and if you can't say THIEF, say nothing at all.'

Richard Grant continues:

> Frankie Aitcheson remembers having a shock wave every time Mrs. Malcom called his name, as she seemed to be ever present correcting his 'broken' English. He also recalls the mango tree at the southwestern corner of the school at Portland Road, which we were forbidden to climb or stone the mangoes. One of the students was stoning the mangoes, and Frankie decided that it would be opportune for him to catch a falling mango. Unfortunately, he did not catch a mango, but instead, a falling rock hit him on his head, causing him to bleed profusely.
>
> He ran to the office for first aid, only to be interrogated after being patched up. Unable, or unwilling to give a detailed account,

he received a few good licks from another teacher, Mrs. MacPherson, called by the students 'Mackitie', only to get another licking at home for disobeying school rules.

Strict discipline was the order of the day in Mrs. Grant's school. Focus was placed on high moral standards, character development, and a deep sense of social duty. Students who attended Camperdown in the forties and fifties remember their Camperdown experience as "happy," "idyllic" and "nurturing." Several remember Miss "Birdie" Taylor, the school's custodian and "Jill of all trades," who also ran the tuck shop selling patties, snow cones and "crust." Miss Birdie's daughter, "Cherry," who attended the school, went on to qualify as an attorney. Winifred Crooks, who later became the first alumna to serve as Principal of the school, remembers "tin lizzie" the Austin 7 motor car that Mrs. Grant drove. "Grantus" was the name that the students called Mrs. Grant, but always with respect and awe, and only out of earshot.

Ivy Grant was always smartly dressed and had a special fondness for linen dresses. She was a strict disciplinarian, stern in countenance. The story is told that when she wore her green or brown linen dress she was stricter than usual. Her presence automatically demanded respect. But beneath all this were the most enduring acts of care, love and affection.

Camperdown was a grand experience in discipline, caring, gumption (a favorite word of Mrs. Grant), responsibility for one's actions, living by the Golden Rule, and embracing the happiness of the experiences. But above all, these were the values instilled in the students by which Camperdown became known. These were largely Christian values of honesty, integrity, discipline, personal deportment, and so on, as exemplified in the school's motto, "Only the best is good enough," and reinforced by daily devotions and term visits to the Lincoln Kirk Presbyterian Church on nearby Lincoln Road.

Mrs. Jean (Pinnock) Bryan served as Head Girl from 1963 – 1964. She attended Camperdown from age three-and-a-half to age 18, from the Kindergarten to the Preparatory, through to the High School. She recalls the

IVY MAY WILSON GRANT—A LIFE OF PURPOSE

dread: "It was a most frightening experience if you were told that Mrs. Grant wanted to see you. You immediately started to ponder on what you might have done. But you had no choice but to report to her office. Well, you made sure that the pleats in your uniform laid flat, your socks and shoes were in proper order, your hair patted down, everything in place. And you dared not enter the office before you were called in. That was Mrs. Grant, a lady of impeccable demeanour."

And Mrs. Cynthia (Warren) Cooke, who attended Camperdown from 1961 – 1966, recalls: "Mrs. Grant was a 'proper' lady. She loathed vulgarity and encouraged good speech at all times. As a Principal, she loved sports, had a special relationship with the boys, and believed in educating the whole child. The quote I will always remember is, 'Mediocre, not a chance, poor, nooooo. It has to be excellent!'"

Camperdown alumni can be found all over the world – doctors, nurses, dentists, engineers, lawyers, bankers, businessmen and women, insurance executives, teachers, university professors, government leaders, public servants, internationally renowned musicians, ambassadors, world class athletes—really, in every endeavour.

Camperdown students were equipped with high moral standards with a clear sense of social duty, and with values that were meant to have meaning in their lives. The school's motto, "ONLY THE BEST IS GOOD ENOUGH," was constantly impressed upon them. That lesson is well imbued!

Ivy Grant always impressed upon her students the need to pursue tertiary education. She, however, never had the opportunity to do likewise in her early years, as her dedication was to her students and the building of Camperdown. She later got the opportunity to do so when the school became a Government-aided high school. In January 1959 she traveled to England to pursue the B.A. degree at the University of London, and succeeded in achieving her goal in 18 months, with credits earned from the years when she pursued the Inter-B.A. She returned to Jamaica in the summer of 1960 and resumed her role as Principal of Camperdown High School in January 1961, where she remained until her retirement in 1968.

A farewell reception for Mrs. Grant was held on Friday, May 24, 1968, at the Flamingo Hotel in Cross Roads.

Between 1971 – 1972, Mrs. Grant was called out of retirement to act as Headmistress of St. Hilda's Diocesan High School in St. Ann. Before that, she lived in New York, where she taught in Brooklyn at the Opportunities Industrialization Center.

True to her motto and to her dedication in improving oneself through education, she also earned a Master's Degree from The City University of New York in 1974 and started work on a second Master's degree in International Educational Development and Adult Education at the Columbia University Teachers College in New York City.

In 1976, the Government of Jamaica recognized Grant's multi-faceted contribution to education by awarding her the Order of Distinction "for service in the field of Education." In 1985, she was posthumously honoured by the country, this time with the award of the Badge of Honour for Long Service in the field of Education. After all, this indomitable woman, Ivy May Wilson Grant, had choreographed Camperdown from a preparatory school to a secondary one, from a girl's high school to a co-educational school, from a private school to an eminent grant-aided school.

In 1981, the President of the Jamaica Teachers' Association, Mr. E.A. Nugent, reflected on perhaps the greatest meaning of Grant's and Camperdown's contribution to the country's history: "…to the children of the black masses, Camperdown emerged on the horizon of the early thirties like a small oasis in a veritable desert of educational opportunities…in its brief existence, Camperdown has expanded into a giant oasis capable of accommodating over 1,500 students."

Ivy Wilson Grant's gift to Jamaica is Camperdown High School. It is said that she was determined to educate everyone, even a fool. She wanted Camperdown to reach the very top with the focus concentrated in one word: EXCELLENCE. Nothing would get her to stop pursuing her dream.

On Tuesday, October 26, 1982, Ivy May Wilson Grant, Founder and First Principal of Camperdown High School, passed away. As a mark of respect, the school was closed on Friday, October 29, 1982. On Sunday, October 31, a Thanksgiving Service for her life was held at the Andrew's Memorial Seventh-day Adventist Church.

Among the speakers at the service were Governor General Sir Florizel

Glasspole, a long-time friend and supporter of the school, who remarked on her foresight, courage and determination, a "woman of stout heart and great determination;" The Honourable Joyce Robinson, a member of the school board; and Mr. F.L. Sangster, former chairman of the school board, who mentioned her outstanding work as an Educator, remarking that "the success of Mrs. Ivy Grant can best be measured by the success of Camperdown." The Honourable A. Wesley Powell, long-time friend, fellow Seventh-day Adventist, and Founder of Excelsior High School and EXED, lauded her as "one of the most outstanding women of our island."

She was interred at Dovecot Memorial Park in St. Catherine.

Tributes to Ivy Grant

Professor Oscar Harriott (As the holder of B.A. and M.A. degrees, he actually joined the staff to bolster the faculty as a grant-aided school. He was a classmate of Ivy Wilson at the West Indies Training College from which he graduated in 1925):

"I never knew a woman with more courage, more determination, and more grit."

Mrs. Winifred (Crooks) Smith – (Class of 1950, who later served as Principal of Camperdown from 1983 to 1992, and Acting Principal 1982-83):

"Mrs. Grant was a dynamic teacher. She was competent, dedicated and inspiring. One was always challenged to produce work that was above average.
I loved Latin! You just had to love Latin if Mrs. Grant taught it.
Mrs. Grant had a vibrant and striking personality.
You would immediately spot her in a room – exuding warmth and vibrancy in life"

THE STORY OF CAMPERDOWN HIGH SCHOOL

Mrs. Irene (Reid) Walter (Class of 1953):

Mrs. Grant was "a dedicated educator who cared deeply for children
who were disadvantaged by the existing system of education.
She was a pioneer in the field of private education, at the time dominated by men.
She was a philanthropist, and a devoted family person.
She believed in the supreme worth of the individual and their right to an education
that would allow for the development of the full potential of the individual.
So many of us benefited from that belief and we are truly grateful.
She not only lived a life that one could emulate, but ensured that she instilled in her charges, values of honesty, caring, independence, determination to succeed and generosity. She was truly a woman of excellence.
Above all, she was a practicing Christian, intuitive and caring.
She had the ability to recognize those students who needed assistance,
whether it was financial support, mentoring or how to apply oneself in order to improve grades. She took the time to address all these."

Mrs. Kathleen Lynch Wilson (taught English, Mathematics and Religious Education at Camperdown in 1945, and friend of 40 years):

"As a friend I found her true and loyal with a strong family tie and a deep and consuming energy to build Camperdown from a private school to a Grant-aided school. She believed in discipline and had a strong faith in the Almighty.
Through Mrs. Grant's generosity many girls and boys received free education.
She was able to employ and keep many excellent and dedicated staff.
Camperdown was held in high profile in East Kingston by Mrs. Grant."

IVY MAY WILSON GRANT—A LIFE OF PURPOSE

Mrs. Nora Malcolm (One of the longest serving members of staff—1933 to 1961):

"We have known and worked together since 1932 and 'nary a moment' of rancor.
We have worked together for 28 years and they have been years of hard work,
but such love and sympathy that there seemed scope for just 'something more.'
She has been untiring in her devotion to duty, indeed, so much that, I for one, thought she would go under. But no, she was always up again and once more to the task of building Camperdown.
Her unfailing exuberance of spirit will long live in the annals of Camperdown and wherever a student of hers resides, here or abroad, each one has caught something of the spark which always radiated from her vibrant personality."

Ms. Carole Reid (Class of 1960):

"Mrs. Grant was the mother figure who knew all her students and, in addition,
she cared for them deeply. For my part, she knew the inadequacies of my parents' resources, and being Mrs. Grant, she organized a private scholarship for me for most of my high school years. Even when I transferred to Excelsior High School for Higher Schools, would you believe it, the scholarship continued! This was the mettle of this wonderful lady. I am certain that my numerous blessings and all that I am today had their genesis in my formative years at Camperdown, not only the high school,
but I was privileged to attend the Kindergarten from age three and a half,
then on to Preparatory school, before moving to the high school. Camperdown was my other family."

2

Going by Faith, Making a Way: 1930s – 1950s

*Now faith is the substance of things hoped for,
the evidence of things not seen.*

(Hebrews 11.1)

The decade of the 1920s was a difficult period for the Jamaican people. Following World War I, the global economy went into a virtual freefall, with a tremendous ripple effect on the local economy. Unemployment was high and rising, wages were low, and hope seemed something of a distant past. The downturn in the economic and social situation deteriorated further with the Great Depression of the late twenties and early thirties, which gave rise to a series of social upheavals across the island in the 1930s.

Between 1934 – 1939, there was significant labour unrest in Jamaica and the rest of the Caribbean. By 1938, dock workers on the Kingston waterfront and workers at Frome Sugar Factory in Westmoreland went on strike, resulting in several deaths during the upheaval of general labour unrest. This led to the formation of the Bustamante Industrial Trade Union (BITU) by Alexander Bustamante, and also to the birth of Jamaica's two main political parties, the People's National Party (PNP), organized by Norman Manley in 1938, and, after Bustamante's break from the PNP, the Jamaica Labour Party (JLP) in 1943.

It was in the harshness of this environment that young Ivy Wilson found herself dreaming, not unlike the many other nationalists of the time, of how to inspire hope and purpose in the people. How could she formulate viable options to improve the lot of the common men and women and to rekindle faith in their country? For deep in the bosom of the ordinary folks of the land was a sad feeling of condemnation, much like Sisyphus', to a social, economic and political burden that seemed to repeat itself endlessly as time progressed.

For the privileged few of the land, these were among the very best of times; for the mass of Black and Brown Jamaicans who comprised the vast majority, it was the worst of times.

Among those who harbored strong nationalist pride, there was the sense that, as difficult as the times were, a big push was needed to raise the possibilities for the future of the people through education. As the 1930s drew to a close, only a minority of Jamaican youth, almost equally divided between girls and boys, attended high school. Less than 3,000 students in the entire country were enrolled in the eleven high schools that were under the control of the Jamaica Schools Commission. These schools primarily served the children of the elite, thereby ensuring the propagation of colonial culture.

It was during this down-trodden time that Ivy Wilson rose to the fore. After separation from her job as Principal of the North Street Seventh-day Adventist School, Ivy found herself at home with nothing much to do. She decided to devote her time to private studies in order to better prepare for the Inter-B.A. degree offered by the University of London. But fate would have it differently!

Thanks to the growing reputation she had built as a first-class educator at the North Street school, family members and neighborhood friends would soon approach her to tutor their children. They needed a tutor to prepare the children for the local scholarship examination in order to win places in the few existing high schools in the country.

So Miss Wilson ultimately agreed to open a school to help achieve this goal. It was only intended to be a short-term solution. She started with four children on the veranda of her father's house at #9 Camperdown Road, at the corner of Camperdown Road and Lincoln Road.

The names of the four students are remembered fondly by Dr. Marcianne Harriott Harris, a long-standing family friend who started in the Prep School and graduated from the high school: Olive Haughton, Dorothy Hayles, Yvette Horton, and Olive Dixon.

THE STORY OF CAMPERDOWN HIGH SCHOOL

The four students did not start school on the same day, but rather on the first two days (February 3 and 4) of the first week in February, 1930.

Miss Wilson's "Home School," opened as a kindergarten and preparatory school, catering to girls and boys up to the age of twelve, with the goal of preparing them to sit the scholarship examination. From ages four to seven, they were placed in the kindergarten section of the school; then they moved to the preparatory section, where they would stay up to the age of twelve. From there, students would be prepared to take the national scholarship examination, guaranteeing a place in one of the top high schools in the country to those who were successful.

Enrollment in Miss Wilson's Home School grew from 4 students to 18 by July of 1930, reaching a total of 40 by October. This made it necessary to move to more spacious surroundings at the family premises on Portland Road. The "Home School" became very popular in the neighborhood and a pride to the residents.

It was a rare delight in the community to see the small, well-behaved children move about in their cute uniform – "Jippi-Jappa" straw hat, navy blue tunic with white blouse and navy blue tie, navy blue socks and black shoes for girls, and khaki pants with white shirt, navy blue tie, navy blue socks and black shoes for boys. In a short time, it was recognized as one of the best kindergarten and preparatory schools in the corporate area.

Yet the early days were not without problems, and there were periods of doubt and indecision. After the first term, Miss Wilson became ill and the school was closed for a period of three months. When she returned, she gave her full attention to increasing enrollment at the school, even as she devoted attention to her own private studies. It was an awesome responsibility, yet after times of doubt and deep reflection, she decided to follow the path to which faith had brought her.

Enrollment expanded rapidly, a true and appropriate reflection of the people's desire for the education of their children. Each succeeding term saw an increase in enrollment. By 1931, the first student to sit the scholarship examination was successful. By 1933, six students sat the exam and four were successful. During that same year, ten students were entered for the Cambridge local examinations; of the ten entered, eight were successful.

Growth at the school continued at a rapid pace. By 1934, a High School section was opened, for girls only. Within two years, a music studio was built as Ivy Wilson embraced a philosophy that music and the fine arts should be an integral part of a young woman's upbringing, a cultured finishing to a girl's education, buttressed with poetry and language. The empowerment of the girls, she was convinced, was of paramount importance if Jamaica was to see positive change. She held firmly to the belief that the country's future depended largely on the strength of the country's womenfolk. She saw discrimination everywhere in society, and many young girls, particularly those of darker complexion in urban areas, could not find a place in Jamaica's then formal educational structure. Access to education at that time was significantly biased in favour of the children of the privileged. Miss Ivy, like many progressive-minded Jamaicans of the period, felt this was a tragic waste of human capital.

A number of other private schools offering secondary learning were organized around this time, exposing the children of the mass to whatever semblance of education they could. These privately-owned schools included Merl Grove (1919), Kingston College (1925), the Excelsior Secondary School (1931), St. Simon's Secondary School (1933), and Buxton High School (1937).

The social stratification system of the country, introduced during the long period of slavery and rigidly reinforced during the colonial years, defined life in the society. In this system, rights and privileges were determined by ascription, from the highest reserved for Whites, to the lowest assigned to Blacks. It was during that era in Jamaica when Gladys Longbridge (later Lady Bustamante) recalled that "since I was not of high complexion, I could not hold a job of any kind in a commercial bank."

The impetus for opening the high school section came from Miss Wilson's realization that many of those young students who were unsuccessful in the scholarship examinations would not gain entry into the grant-aided schools. Thus, they would be denied the opportunity of gaining a secondary education, and then be faced with dwindling chances of future expectations despite potential. Given the very limited number of available spaces in the traditional high schools, and thus a limited number of awards to these schools, many qualified students were intentionally "failed." So, at the frenetic request of many parents, particularly those at the lower echelon of the society, Miss

Wilson opened the way forward for these students in 1934. Fees were affordable to most parents, which also helped to attract wider support for the school. The academic programme did not go beyond Senior Cambridge, yet it offered exceptional tutelage. Teachers and students blended as family. The message she sought to convey was rather simple, yet forceful: *if they had the WILL, she would provide the WAY.*

And find a way she did! In 1930s Jamaica, the curriculum at Miss Wilson's school focused on more than just the traditional grammar school (liberal education) offerings (the three R's – reading, 'riting, 'rithmetic, etc.). It also included the more "practical" subjects of Home Economics, Cookery, Needlework, and commercial subjects. Miss Wilson's students were exposed to a magnificent music programme, including singing, dancing, and arts. There was percussion band and Eistedfodd. There was also keep-fit dancing to groom "perfect little ladies." Moreover, Camperdown's curriculum included Latin and Spanish – the only preparatory school teaching Latin and Spanish in Jamaica at the time.

Ivy Grant embarked on a journey to provide opportunities and to instill in her young charges the sense of leadership, pride, spirit of cooperation, creativity, joy, and discipline needed to confront adversity in their lives. A Camperdown education, Ivy Grant reasoned in those early days, was "not geared solely at passing Cambridge exams, but rather at ensuring that our students had character, morality, and worth, therefore every student who came up through the school received a school-leaving certificate."

The early Camperdown years—of the 1930s to the 1950s—were essentially geared to prepare students with marketable skills for the Civil Service, teaching and commercial pursuits. Many of those early students went on to distinguish themselves in a variety of fields, both locally and abroad.

The new initiatives and accumulated successes gave rise to new problems, as soon the high school facilities proved inadequate. To cope with a steadily increasing population of students, Miss Ivy used a mix of resoluteness coupled with her strong Christian beliefs.

Creative arrangements were made to find additional space by adjoining the family-owned properties at #16 and #16A Portland Road. Some of the younger students were sent back to her father's veranda at Camperdown Road to continue classes.

Throughout the 1930s and the early years of the 1940s, Miss Wilson's school was referred to as the "Camperdown School" or as "Camperdown Girl School." The name "Camperdown High School," used in reference to Miss Wilson's school, did not come into popular use until much later. All sporting activities in which the school was engaged referred to the "Camperdown School" and "Camperdown Girl School." This essentially continued until the mid-1940s after the opening of the new building at #16-1/2 Portland Road. Much of the advertisements for the school between 1931 and 1937 made reference to the "Home School." An advertisement in **The Gleaner** newspaper (December 24, 1931) noted the wider exposure students would get at the Home School, now offering music education "with exceptionally qualified teachers." By 1935 a music studio was opened and students were welcomed to the "Home School" at 16A Portland Road, where they would be prepared not only for the "foundation scholarships and Cambridge Locals," but also for the "School Certificate and Junior Examinations" and the "musical exams of the Royal School of Music."

The expansion in the High School section of the school was similar to Camperdown Girl School's early success, and increased visibility soon called for a building-expansion programme. Financing growth and development in the especially difficult environment of the day called for personal sacrifice, a drain on family resources, winning community support, the sacrifice of staff, and endless fundraising events. Ivy Grant recalled how this was managed in a later interview:

> So I went down to Hardware and Lumber (the local hardware mega-store in downtown Kingston) on King Street. I was recommended by Mr. George Rennie. [There] I got Fifty Pounds Ten Shillings and Seven Pence credit, to facilitate my expansion. When my father heard I had gone and gotten into debt, he was astounded and went and paid it all off, which only opened the way for further credit. The manager Mr. DeMercado was very impressed by my

promptness in settling my debts, and called it to the attention of his staff…Camperdown was my first child."

Additional space also became available as some of the older girls in the high school section took classes at the nearby Lucas Cricket Club, located at the corner of St. James Road and Preston Road.

To finance the expansion of facilities and course offerings, etc., numerous fund-raising initiatives were pursued – bake sales, barn dances, students' collection drives, Miss Wilson's favorite tea parties—as well as encouraging philanthropic contributions. On May 1, 1943 the school sponsored a Barn Dance held at the Lucas Pavilion "in aid of their School Extension Fund" and, according to **The Daily Gleaner** of May 4, "it was a hearty success." Music for the occasion was provided by the Caribbean Orchestra, which, the report goes on to say, "was in tip-top form." At this stellar event, "the best ladies' costume was worn by Miss Daphne Bennett, who made a pretty Gipsy (sic) girl, and Mrs. Ivy Bell, who came delightfully dressed as a country maid. Mr. Thoywell Henry as an estate headman wore the best male costume." Additionally, the Old Students' Association held numerous events to help fund the school, including the acquisition of a well-needed playfield.

Miss Wilson (by now Mrs. Grant) worked tirelessly, not only to build the school, but to cultivate support from the wider society. Her time was spent not only on scholarship and teaching, but now managing a growing business, supervising staff, upgrading facilities, and shouldering responsibility for everything from advertising to marketing in promoting the school and its possibilities. In the relentless push to "sell" her school, Miss Wilson was a tireless campaigner. Some of the most prominent citizens in the country in public life and business could be seen at Camperdown events. Numbered among them were: Councillor Mrs. Mary Morris-Knibb; Hon. E.A. Campbell, a leading barrister and trade unionist; Mr. Evon Blake, noted journalist; Miss Amy Bailey, noted educator and activist; Mr. J.E. Clare McFarlane, President of the Poetry League of Jamaica and, in later years, the country's second Poet Laureate; Mr. Herbert Anglin Jones, legendary Head Teacher of the Rollington Town Primary School; Mr. and Mrs. George Goode (Jamaica Military Band); Mr. F. A. Glasspole, trade unionist and politician; and Mr. Merrick McGilchrist, businessman.

"As busy as a bee," as the saying goes, Ivy Grant found time to serve as

GOING BY FAITH, MAKING A WAY: 1930s – 1950s

Treasurer of the Jamaica Independent Schools' Association (a union of private secondary high schools), a position to which she was elected unopposed for several years. The association consisted of Excelsior College, Normal College, Tutorial Secondary School, Waltham College, Carlyle College, St. Mary's High School, Cosmopolitan High School, Merl Grove High School, St. James High School, and Camperdown High School. Despite these fast-paced activities, scholarship continued to soar, and each year Camperdown students were numbered among the island's top scholarship winners.

The teaching staff was also making notable strides, and in July 1939 the school held an impressive farewell tea party in honour of one of its outstanding teachers, Miss Linda Edwards. She taught Spanish at the school from 1937 to 1939, and was the winner of the Jamaica's first Issa scholarship to study Art in London. The July 20, 1939 issue of **The Daily Gleaner** reported on the event, noting "the pride and joy" of Miss Edwards, who "was presented by the school with a writing case made of Tooled leather on English calf and with a design of native wild flowers, the work of Miss Gwen Sinclair," a teacher at the school.

Miss Amy Bailey, a guest speaker at the event and one of the leaders in the struggle for social, economic and political rights at the time, said that "the recent 'Upheaval' had played a large part in opening the eyes of others to the fact that we [the Black majority] ought to get a chance…and was convinced that others would have been able to do the same [as Miss Edwards] if similar opportunities had been offered."

In an effort to raise the awareness of the students and prepare them for the world they would inherit, many prominent speakers were invited to address the students. Among them was Mrs. Amy Jacques Garvey, a close friend of Mrs. Grant and wife of Mr. Marcus Garvey. Mrs. Garvey would visit the school each term to lecture to the students on African History, pride in self and heritage, and the importance of acquiring a sound education. Her talks were spiced with much of Garvey's aphorisms, such as, "If you have no confidence in self, you are twice defeated in the race of life." Mrs. Merle (Wilson) Meeks, who attended Camperdown during the 1940s, remembers how captivated the students were listening to Mrs. Garvey: "And we would pay close attention to all that was imparted to us, sitting on the edge of our chairs in awe."

The visits of these prominent speakers, "live and direct," was intended to provide role models so the students could see a reflection of themselves and dream to a more glorious future.

Back in 1938, of the few scholarships offered for places in the few elite high schools, four Camperdown students were awarded a total of six scholarships. Louis Lewis, won a full scholarship to St. George's College; nine-year-old Joy Chen won a full scholarship to St. Andrew High School for Girls; nine-year-old Muriel Lowe won a full scholarship to St. Andrew High School, as well as an Exhibition Scholarship to Wolmer's Girls School; and ten-year-old Zita Haughton also won a full scholarship to St. Andrew High School and an Exhibition Scholarship to Wolmer's Girls School. Understandably, the little "Home School" was beaming with pride at these successes.

Muriel Lowe went on to St. Andrew High School. In 1948 she was one of the ten female students selected from throughout the English-speaking Caribbean that formed the inaugural class of 33 to start the newly-opened medical school at the University College of the West Indies at Mona, Jamaica.

Many other success stories helped to lift the profile of the school and propel it into the further consciousness of the society. On December 28, 1940, ten-year-old Norma Miller from Camperdown Girl School was highlighted in *The Daily Gleaner* as a "brilliant scholar" after winning two scholarships – one for Wolmer's Girls School and the other for St. Andrew High School. In that same year, eight other scholarship awards were won by Camperdown students, including Marjorie Lewis and Fay White to Alpha Academy, Barbara Gibson to the Immaculate Conception High School, and Marjorie Stanton to Wolmer's Girls School.

In addition to academic success, sports were also an integral part of the school's curriculum. In 1937, Camperdown Girl School, entering the meet for the first time, finished in 9th place in the second annual Private Secondary Schools Track and Field meet at Kensington Park. *The Daily Gleaner* (May 7, 1940) also noted the "Camperdown Girl School's" participation in the 1940 Private Secondary Schools' Track and Field championships sports at Sabina Park, which included first-timers St. Simon's College and St. Martin's High School, both co-ed schools, and two all-girls' schools, Camperdown and Merl Grove. "Camperdown Girls' School" also participated in the Women's Amateur Athletic Association's inaugural sports meet, held at Sabina Park on June 25 and 26 of the same year. A team representing Camperdown Old Girls also participated in the relay races.

GOING BY FAITH, MAKING A WAY: 1930s – 1950s

By 1943, the "Camperdown Girl School" placed 4th in the meet held at Sabina Park, in the process setting a new Jamaica schoolgirl record in the 4x75 yards relay. Barbara King, a Class 3 athlete, won the prize for "most determined effort, courage and spirit." A Camperdown boys' team was also entered in the meet for the first time, wearing the school's colour—blue and white.

At the same time, the school maintained its lofty standing in preparing students for the scholarship examinations. Camperdown students to whom scholarships were awarded in 1942 were listed in an advertisement in **The Daily Gleaner** (January 5, 1943): Norma Lee to Hampton [Girls] School; Patricia Chen to Wolmer's Girls School; Ronald Chen to Kingston College; Alston Bain to Wolmer's Boys School; George Wong to Tutorial College; and Pearl Codling to Happy Grove College. The advertisement served as a reminder to the parents that the new school term would begin on Monday, January 11.

These continuing successes placed the school on a roll and the demand for acceptance to the school far exceeded the available resources. To cope with the necessary expansion and the need for additional teachers, it became necessary to raise the school fees. A number of fundraising events were also held by the old students. Despite this, it was Ivy Grant's mandate that no child would be denied a place in her school for lack of tuition.

But even while coping with the rapid pace of fundraising and expansion, the school remained actively involved in sports. Although the school continued to participate in the Secondary Schools Track and Field meets, ironically, it was not until 1943 that the school held its first sports day at Nelson Oval with competition among the three houses in a variety of events, including "Lime and Spoon race," "Handkerchief race," "Potato race," and "Needle and Thread race." At the Private Secondary Track and Field meet in March of 1944 at Sabina Park, the Camperdown Girl School (C.G.S.) athletes were adorned in the school's new colors: navy blue, silver, and white. Camperdown also participated in the Jamaica Independent Secondary Schools Track and Field Championship for girls, scoring two successes, both in Class 3 – Barbara King, 3rd in the 150-yard race, and 2nd in the 4x75 yards relay. Later in the year (on September 25), the school presented "A Pageant of the United Nations and the Nations in Bondage," in concert with the Jamaica Military Band at Lucas Club and at Hope Gardens.

THE STORY OF CAMPERDOWN HIGH SCHOOL

During 1944, from September to December, there was a temporary relocation of the school to premises at 11 Camperdown Road in order to accommodate the construction of the new school building at Portland Road.

◈

On Tuesday, February 20, 1945, the new and very imposing Camperdown School building at 16-1/2 Portland Road was formally opened and dedicated. This day was described as one of the happiest days in Ivy Grant's life. The school's choir, under the direction of music master George Goode, opened the occasion with the school's song, "We Would Be True." By the following year, **The Sunday Gleaner** (November 17, 1946) made reference to the new building as "one of the most imposing of its kind in the entire island."

Advertisements celebrating the new building made note of the opening of a Commercial Department offering "Shorthand, Typing, Elementary Book-keeping, Commercial English, Mathematics, and Office Deportment." Evening/Extension classes were added with hours from 5pm to 8pm.

The affair marking the opening of the new building was rather impressive. The building was described as "an imposing appearance, very spacious and well ventilated." The second floor included an assembly hall, where school events as well as daily devotion were held. Attendees at the opening numbered a veritable "Who's Who" in Jamaica: His Worship the Mayor, Alderman William Seivright and Mrs. Seivright; Member of the House of Representative for the East Kingston constituency, Mr. F.A. Glasspole and Mrs. Glasspole; Reverend Father Gladstone Wilson, prominent Roman Catholic priest, then considered one of the brightest persons in the world; the Moderator of the Presbyterian Church in Jamaica, Rev. C.M. Watler; Rev. Canon Walter Brown, who dedicated the building; Rev. Canon E.L. Evans; Councillor Mary Morris Knibb; Mr. F.A. Myers; Mr. George Goode, the leader of the Jamaica Military Band, and Mrs. Goode; Mrs. E.E. Ranger-Jones, Headmistress of the Windsor High School; Dr. and Mrs. Hugh K. Lloyd; Rev. Ivan Francis, Headmaster of Lincoln and Business Colleges; Mr. Ruel N. Vaz; Mr. and Mrs. Harold Brown; Dr. E.H. Evans and Miss Evans; Mr. H. Anglin Jones, Secretary

GOING BY FAITH, MAKING A WAY: 1930s – 1950s

of the Jamaica Union of Teachers and Principal of the Rollington Town Elementary School, and Mrs. Jones; Mr. H. McD. Messam; Mrs. E. Dalton James; Mrs. Ivy Bell; and Mr. and Mrs. E.A. Grant. The occasion was presided over by Mr. J.J. Mills, the acting Principal of the Mico Training College. Music for the occasion was provided by the Caribbean Orchestra.

Ivy Grant's Christian calling was reflected in her speech and she attributed the school's success to the Lord: "And so to Him, who has guided us through the past fifteen years, we humbly dedicate this new phase of Camperdown's growth, confident that the everlasting arms will continue to uphold us yesterday, today and tomorrow."

The school's outreach in the community was also reflected in the fact that throughout the 1940s the school premises were used to host a number of civic events, such as an annual Christmas treat for indigent children from Rollington Town, meetings of community groups, and evening classes hosted by the Extra Mural Department of the University College of the West Indies.

In the month following the opening of the new building, on March 28, 1945, the school held its annual Eisteddfod. Students were judged in a number of areas, such as national dancing, elocution, singing and percussion band, as well as the year's school work, in games, housecraft and needlework. There was intense competition between the three houses—Aggrey, Dickens and Washington.

The day's activities, as always, started with the singing of the school's song, "We Would Be True," and included competition in songs, country dancing, recitation, pianoforte selections and choruses. Aggrey House won the cup by two points over Washington House. Special awards were given to students Iris Webster for the best essay on "Insurance," and Jacqueline Stanton for "outstanding graciousness." Dickens House emerged winners of the Netball Cup.

One should also not forget the famous Tenequoit (Deck Tennis/Ring Tennis) competition between the houses.

The school continued to grow in popularity, but the demand for available spaces far exceeded the supply. So, by 1951, two more classrooms were built, followed by more classrooms in 1956. Land was also acquired at #4 Camperdown Road for use as a playing field, a pressing need as the school's lack of adequate playing areas was deemed a constraint in the school's performance in the sporting arena. To help remedy the situation, the Old Students' Association held various fundraising activities.

Camperdown Girl School was highly regarded among the top secondary schools of the period, certainly the very best of the growing number of private secondary schools. The school's annual prize-giving was a masterfully crafted event. This was the occasion at which the "Camperdown ladies" were presented to the wider society, much akin to the Cotillion balls then popular in the United States and the debutante balls at Buckingham Palace, where young women were "presented." The Camperdown young ladies, all ceremoniously dressed in white and with prior instructions in social etiquette and appropriate morals, would make their appearances with crisp movements to the delight of all.

Merle Meeks remembers how impressed she was when, as a thirteen-year-old girl, she first encountered this prize-giving event upon entering Camperdown. "I had long wanted to be a Camperdown girl. I entered the school during the nineteen forties. I remember that very well. I was in love with the uniform, pleated Navy Blue skirt, white blouse, and blue tie and the Jippi-Jappa hat." She recalled a few of the girls who were at Camperdown when she was there, and named Ena Meeks, Olive Dixon – who went on to study medicine at Howard University in the United States, Dorothy Hayles and Claire Dixon, one of the many girls who came to Camperdown via the Kingston Senior School (now Kingston High School).

Mrs. Meeks also recalled some of the boys then at the school – Julius Garvey, son of Marcus Garvey. After leaving Camperdown Preparatory School, he attended Wolmer's Boys School and later studied medicine in Canada. Then there were the Girvan boys, the Dewdney boys, Dennis Repole, Junior Kirkwood, Ronald Manderson-Jones and Ryan Peralto. Trevor Dewdney went on to Calabar High School and later qualified as a Veterinary Doctor. Dennis (Denny) Repole became a leading Architect, and Ryan Peralto went on to St. George's College, entered politics and served as Mayor of Kingston/St. Andrew and also as a Member of Parliament. Manderson-Jones went on to Jamaica College, and thereafter studied law and became a diplomat and author. Ivy Grant's son, Richard, moved on to Jamaica College; the two sons of Professor Harriott—Chester and Oscar, Jr.—and Adrian Wallace, went to Calabar. Wallace was instrumental in bringing the 2002 World Junior Athletics Championships to Jamaica. Colin Tyrie went to St. George's

College, while his sister, Lorna Tyrie (later Mrs. Lorna Peralto), stayed on in the high school at Camperdown. The school nurtured a host of promising boys who went on to excel as professionals and helped to build the profile of other high schools. Many are numbered among the most prominent men in the building and development of a greater Jamaican nation.

Colin Tyrie recalls that during the 1940s, a large number of the students at Camperdown (about 60 per cent) had Chinese surnames.

Camperdown remained in the news through its scholarship. In July 1956, it was announced that Walter Wong, who in 1949 went to Calabar High School after winning a scholarship from Camperdown Prep School, had won the first award of the coveted Yap Sam Scholarship to study medicine at the University College of the West Indies (now the University of the West Indies).

Many of the older girls who attended Camperdown High School came via St. Michael's School on Tower Street. There was, in fact, a working pipeline between St. Michael's and Camperdown, given the close relationship between teachers at both schools, and Camperdown was seen as a natural conduit to secondary education for many of these girls from humble Jamaican families. These students came well prepared; many of them already held passes at the First and Second Jamaica Local examinations, taken by many outside the few elite high schools.

It is to the credit of these girls that they would walk the three miles from St. Michael's to the Kingston Senior School at Upper King Street, near Race Course (now called National Heroes Park) to take the extra classes to prepare for these examinations. These girls, among the best and brightest in the country, included Winifred Crooks and her sister, Norma Crooks, Shirley Smith, Patricia Paul, Joyce Moore, Emen Donaldson and Hilma McCalla.

Notable among them also was Irene Reid [later Mrs. Irene Walter] who came to Camperdown on scholarship in 1950 after passing the Third Jamaica Local Examination at age 14, placing third in the island. In 1953, she passed the Cambridge School Certificate examination in Grade 1, and then went on to Excelsior High School to do the Higher School Examination.

THE STORY OF CAMPERDOWN HIGH SCHOOL

The atmosphere at Camperdown during the 1940s was one of family. There were siblings, cousins, nieces and nephews, and sons and daughters of teachers. Mrs. Grant's nieces, Kay and Claudette Wilson, both attended, from the preparatory to the high school. A few of the students from rural areas boarded with Mrs. Grant, with teachers or with other family members.

The school was noted for its emphasis on music, and the school's choir was consistently placed among the top three in schools' competition. Students had a passion for work; school spirit was contagious. Dr. Marcianne Harriott Harris remembers well those years:

> I can never forget my very first day at Camperdown. I was but four years old. I was not afraid to go to school that day as any four year old might have been, because Miss Ivy May Wilson (she was not yet married to Mr. Norman Grant) was the Headmistress of Camperdown and a long-time friend of my father and my mother…
>
> And how quickly did the years come and go, gliding like shuttles through the loom of time weaving the fabric of our destinies. I spent all of my early school years at Camperdown as well as through to my teenage years, proudly and happily passing my Senior Cambridge exams. The academic programme did not go beyond Senior Cambridge then, but offered exceptional tutelage…There was hardly a dull day at Camperdown. Mr. George Goode taught us to sing. Mrs. Grant was a good singer herself. What a great music department! Then, there was Mr. Bob Stewart (Uncle Bob), Director of the Jamaica Military Band that came to play for us at Eisteddfod time, as well as Sargeant Major Beckett from Up Park Camp. There was Drama and Dancing around the Maypole, directed by Miss Girvan.
>
> I can remember participating in Shakespearian plays like "As You Like It" and "A Midsummer's Night's Dream" and others, and performing at Up Park Camp Jamboree when the Queen of England visited Jamaica. Mrs. McPherson taught us Mathematics and Mrs. Burke taught Spanish and Mathematics. These two teachers were the best…Mrs. Malcolm taught us all the literature we could remember–Shakespeare, Wordsworth, and Health Science. Mrs. Lindo was our Art teacher. Mrs. McFarlane was our music teacher. Mrs. Grant herself offered English Language and Latin.

Lower School was from Kindergarten to IV-B Junior (Prep School and co-ed). The Upper School was forms IV-A, V-B, V-A (high school for girls only)…The school family was divided into three competitive "Houses"—Aggrey House – leader, Mrs. Malcolm and the colour Blue; Dickens House – leader, Mrs. Burke and the colour pink; and Washington House – leader, Mrs. McPherson and the colours gold and purple. Students in these houses engaged in healthy rivalry.…

The religious aspect of our school life was never neglected. Every morning before classes the school family gathered for worship, where there was group singing of hymns and prayers. I cannot forget it since it was I, in those days, who played the piano as we sang our praises to God. Others who accompanied on the piano were Dorothy Hayles, Sheila Burke, Barbara Murphy, Rita Hypolite and Maxine Franklin. On Wednesday afternoon of each week there was "Youth Fellowship" gatherings with Reverend [Douglas] Miller from the Presbyterian Church and Mrs. Grant leading out as the students worshipped. I remember Shirley Smith, one of our students, leading out quite often. She was quite religious.

Student-led worship was an important part of life at Camperdown. The religious and family foundation undergirded the character of the school. Favourite hymns included "The King of Love, My Shepherd Is," "Angel Voices Ever Singing," "All Things Bright and Beautiful," and "Eternal Father, Strong to Serve." Maxine Franklin went on to become an internationally renowned classical pianist.

In 1948, Camperdown students gave a singing recital at Hope Gardens, working in concert with the Jamaica Military Band. The event was greeted with much "public" acclaim.

In 1953, the graduating class was addressed by the Honourable Philip Sherlock, Vice-Principal of the University College of the West Indies, one of the foremost intellectuals in the country. He encouraged the students that steadfastness and hope were to be their watchword, and that, as they faced the world, their best preparation would be "inborn intelligence, courage and hope." Prayer was offered by Reverend Douglas Miller. Hyacinth King was crowned "Girl of the Class of 1952," selected by classmates as the most outstanding girl in the graduating class.

THE STORY OF CAMPERDOWN HIGH SCHOOL

Reverend Miller was an early supporter of the young neighbourhood school, and played a most prominent role in its early years. When the school came under the auspices of the Presbyterian Church, he was chosen as the first chairman of the school board. Miller House was established to honour the immense influence he wielded in bringing the school to grant-aided status and in its later development.

Marcianne Harriott Harris also recalls one of the famous quotes Mrs. Grant often delivered to her female students: "Ladies, you have heard the famous saying – when in Rome you do as the Romans. No, no, she said, when in Rome you do as the BEST Roman, since your BEST Roman will always do the RIGHT thing."

Camperdown changed uniform colours in the mid-fifties, moving from the traditional navy-blue and white to the colours that came to define the school, cocoa-brown and white – brown pleated tunic (skirts) with spotless white blouse, brown shoes and socks, and fitted with a cocoa-brown beret (tam). According to Mrs. Grant, the choice of the colours was made by the staff and senior prefects. When the school became a grant-aided institution in 1958 the uniform remained the same for the girls. With "bigger" boys now in the mix, the uniform for boys was a khaki shirt and pants, with brown and white epaulettes.

In 1956, Dr. Ena Thomas, a past student of the school who had recently earned her medical degree, presented the graduates with their certificates in a very imposing ceremony. Prizes were also awarded for "Christian Piety and Virtue." Annette FitzRitson was chosen as "Girl of the Class of 1956."

※

During the 1950s, Camperdown established its pedigree in the Secondary School Softball League, playing against schools as Immaculate Conception High School, Kingston Technical School, Excelsior High School, Waulgrove College, Merl Grove High School, Tutorial College, Buxton High School, Alpha Academy, Crescent High School and Grantham College.

At the preparatory level, the record shows the young boys playing a cricket match against the Morris Knibb School in 1951. Camperdown lost!

In 1957, Hermine Jones was named as "Girl of the Year."

GOING BY FAITH, MAKING A WAY: 1930s – 1950s

In the 1957 softball season (their first in the league and playing under coach Roy Archer) the Camperdown girls were crowned the Secondary Schoolgirls Softball League champions. The following year (1958) they lost the league crown and were runners-up to Buxton High School. In the Knockout Championship that same year, Camperdown defeated Buxton by a score of 14-8. They again defeated Buxton in a special presentation game at the end of the season. Camperdown was again the Knockout champion in 1959.

Camperdown produced many outstanding female athletes during the 1950s, particularly in Softball and Track and Field. During this period, Camperdown was known as a powerhouse in girls' softball.

Among Camperdown's outstanding softball players of the period were Claire Dixon, Fay Johnson, Yvonne Hill, Beatrice McDonald, Eleanor Hutton, Beatrice Smith, Emma McMasters and Annie Golding, described as "the woman with the bullet-like throw who packs a mighty wallop in her hits." The All-Schools team named by the Jamaica Amateur Softball Association for the 1959 season included three Camperdown girls in the 9-player starting team – Annie Golding at First Base, Emma McMasters at Short Stop, and Fay Johnson at Center Field. Awards were won by McMasters for "Best Batting Average" and Golding for "Runs Batted In."

In 1959, at the first annual track and field meet of the new co-ed school, Annie Golding received the McD. Messam Cup for the champion girl, while Hubert Hicks received the Sangster Cup as champion boy. At the annual West Indies Track and Field Athletic Championships (1960), 18-year old Annie Golding and another Camperdown student, 17-year old Ethlyn Smith, represented Jamaica. Golding was a triple gold medalist (Shot Put, Discus, Javelin), and was named as the outstanding female athlete of the Championship. Smith won the silver medal in the 80-metres hurdles.

In November, 1959, in the annual Musical Competition Festival among primary and secondary schools, the Camperdown School choir won the trophy in the 15-plus category. They were highly commended by the judges for their expressive interpretation and clear diction.

The house system was also realigned; the three new houses were: Glasspole House (named for the Honourable Florizel Glasspole—colour gold); Grant House (named for Mrs. Grant—colour red); and Miller House (named for Reverend Miller – colour royal blue).

THE STORY OF CAMPERDOWN HIGH SCHOOL

Annie Golding, the school's first multi-event athlete and Head Girl for 1959 (the top female student leader), was one of the foremost female athletes in the country. She was a national representative in track and field and was captain of the Jamaica Softball Team. She also held the West Indies female record in the Discus.

In 1960, Golding was named as Jamaica's "Sportswoman of the Year."

As the 1950s came to a close, after almost three decades at the helm of the school, with enormous challenges and sacrifices, financial as well as personal, Ivy Grant came to the conclusion that the future of her beloved High School could no longer be assured without outside intervention. Financing the growth and development of the school during the three decades of its existence called for continued sacrifices, family resources, community support, sacrifice of staff and family, and frequent fund-raising events as concerts, plays, and fairs. Overall, those took a toll.

By 1958, the school had grown to almost 300 students and resources were difficult to come by. The pressing problem was trying to accommodate the students in the five classrooms built on a quarter acre of land. Acting upon her deep Christian faith, Ivy Grant wanted her school to be aligned with the church. The nearby Lincoln Kirk Presbyterian Church under the leadership of Reverend Miller (who served at the Lincoln Kirk Church from 1949 – 1966) was approached and discussions were entered into with the Synod of the Presbyterian Church of Jamaica (later called The United Church in Jamaica and The Cayman Islands). These discussions took place at an opportune time as the Presbyterian Church was also in the process of expanding its educational activities.

The Reverend Ashley Smith, husband of Mrs. Winifred Smith, was a senior officer of the United Church hierarchy in Jamaica and later an Advisor to the Prime Minister of Jamaica during the 1970s. He mentions that the Presbyterian Church at the time (during the 1950s) was focused on developing schools as St. Andrew High School, Meadowbrook High School, Knox College and Iona High School. The talks between Mrs. Grant and the Church were fruitful and an agreement was reached whereby the church would take over ownership of the school. The school would move from personal ownership to church ownership. The Church thus provided funding to purchase the largest available property in the community – four and a half acres of land with a very large wooden house at 6B Camperdown Road, owned by the Isaacs family. After refurbishing the building and the construction of some outer classrooms, in September, 1958, Camperdown High School was opened as a Government-aided, co-educational school under the auspices of the Presbyterian Church of Jamaica.

THE STORY OF CAMPERDOWN HIGH SCHOOL

A Pictorial Journey (1930s – 1950s)

[Courtesy of Camperdown High School]
The family house at #9 Camperdown Road provided the veranda where the school started in 1930

GOING BY FAITH, MAKING A WAY: 1930s – 1950s

[Courtesy of Camperdown High School]
Around the Maypole—'Fun Day' at the Camperdown School (Portland Road)

[Courtesy of Camperdown High School]
School picture of the pioneering students of the Camperdown School (Circa early 1930's)

THE STORY OF CAMPERDOWN HIGH SCHOOL

[Courtesy of Camperdown High School]
These 3 girls from the Camperdown School – Muriel Lowe, Joy Chen, Zita Haughton— won a total of five scholarships in the 1938 Scholarship Examinations

[Courtesy of Camperdown High School]
1940 Scholarship Winners— (back row l/r) Marjorie Lewis, Fay White; (front row l/r) Barbara Gibson, Marjorie Stanton

[Courtesy of Camperdown High School]
Graduating class of Camperdown High School (December 1953)

GOING BY FAITH, MAKING A WAY: 1930s – 1950s

[Courtesy of Camperdown High School]
Camperdown Debutantes (Circa early 1950s)

[Courtesy of Camperdown High School]
The new Camperdown High School building—
16 ½ Portland Road (1945)
In front of the building is a group of students and teachers

THE STORY OF CAMPERDOWN HIGH SCHOOL

[Courtesy of Camperdown High School]
Dignitaries at opening of new building – 16 ½ Portland Road (1945) (front left to right) Rev. C. M. Watler, Moderator of the Presbyterian Church in Jamaica; Mrs. Ivy M. Grant (Headmistress); His Worship, The Mayor Alderman William Seivright; Mrs. Seivright; Mr. J. J. Mill, Acting Principal of the Mico Training Cottage; (back left to right) Rev. Canon Walter Brown; Mr. H. Anglin Jones; Mr. Florizel Glasspole

GOING BY FAITH, MAKING A WAY: 1930s – 1950s

[Courtesy of Camperdown High School]
*Mrs. Ivy Grant (second right) with patrons
and supporters at fundraising tea party (Circa 1940s)*

[Courtesy of Camperdown High School]
*Mrs. Ivy Grant (second left)—Founder/Headmistress,
with Camperdown High School teachers
Mrs. Muriel Barclay (left), Mrs. Nora Malcom (second right) and Mrs.
G. Lindo (far right) (Circa late 1940s]*

THE STORY OF CAMPERDOWN HIGH SCHOOL

[Courtesy of Camperdown High School]
These six students of Camperdown Preparatory School won seven scholarships to high schools in the 1953 Scholarship Examinations Sitting (left), C. Lyn (St. Hugh's and Manchester High School); Sitting (right, K. Myers (St. Andrew High School)
Standing (left), J. Aitcheson (Happy Grove High School); Standing (center), C. Gooden (St. Andrew High School)
Standing (right), M. Burke (St. Hugh's High School), and Roy Hew (Calabar High School)

GOING BY FAITH, MAKING A WAY: 1930s – 1950s

[Courtesy of Camperdown High School]
Emma McMasters – star Shortstop of Camperdown's championship softball team (1959)

[Courtesy of Camperdown High School]
Annie Golding – Camperdown's first super athlete (track & field and softball) (1959)

3

Major Building Years: 1960s – 1970s

September 1958 came with a huge surge of energy and excitement, and the atmosphere at the school was dominated with a flurry of activities. Grant-aided status had arrived with expectations of many and new possibilities. Arrangements had to be put in place to facilitate the move from Portland Road to the new premises at 6B Camperdown Road. By the end of December, all arrangements were in place to begin the New Year (1959) at the Camperdown Road campus.

On December 12, the school was declared open by Mrs. Florizel Glasspole, wife of the Member of the House of Representatives for the area in which the school was located. The Moderator of the Presbyterian Church, Reverend Henry Ward, did the dedication. Mrs. Grant delivered a major address on the history of the school and the way forward. The new Camperdown happily joined the list as one of only 34 grant-aided secondary schools in the country. It was listed officially as a "mixed-day" co-educational Government secondary school.

Camperdown's location in East Kingston meant that eligible students from areas such as Rollington Town, Franklin Town, Rockfort, Bournemouth Gardens, Newton Square, Rae Town, Brown's Town, and downtown Kingston, plus outlying communities as Norman Gardens, Vineyard Town, and Mountain View, would now be able to access high school education in a relatively close-by area. This was much easier (and less expensive, too) than travelling many miles to other grant-aided schools in the Kingston and St. Andrew administrative region. But under the circumstances of the period,

MAJOR BUILDING YEARS: 1960s – 1970s

Camperdown also became the school of destiny for many students from faraway, disadvantaged communities.

A number of changes were made in order to accommodate the newfound grant-aided status. First, the physical facilities and amenities now had to cater to boys over the age of twelve. Classroom arrangements had to accommodate the new co-ed situation. The atmosphere was brimful of high and hitherto unthought-of expectations.

Among the first order of business to get the school going was the organization of a Board of Governors. The first school Board was comprised of 15 members: 13 chosen by the church, and two by the Government. A number of prominent businesspersons were selected. The members were: Rev. Douglas R. Miller, Chairman and Chaplain; Mr. F.L. Sangster, Vice-Chairman: Rev. H.G. Williams; Rev. A. Henry; Rev. M. Carrick; Mr. H. Malcolm; Mr. R. Keizs; Mr. Lister Mair; Mr. H. McD. Messam; Mr. F.A. Douce; Mrs. Wilson; Miss M. Saunders; Miss M. Thomas; Miss Jean MacNee, Secretary and Bursar; and the Headmaster.

Camperdown's entry into co-ed reality reflected the Government's focus on education. The administration of Premier Norman Manley presented ambitious plans to advance the country through a new emphasis on education. By 1957, the government had developed plans to rapidly increase the number of places in high schools through the Common Entrance Examination and a reform of free placements in the entire system. The Common Entrance Examination allowed an expanded number of students from poorer backgrounds to now attend a grant-supported high school, with fees paid by the government. Many new schools were envisioned in these new plans. The new focus to move the nation forward through education reform called for an expansion of available choices and places in the high school system. To this end, 2,000 additional "free places" were added to the Government-aided roster of high schools through the Common Entrance Examination. Among the new schools that also acquired grant-aid status during the late 1950s were Oberlin High School, Glenmuir High School, York Castle High School, St. Catherine High School, Meadowbrook High School, St. Mary's College, and St. Mary High School.

As remarkable as this might seem looking back from today's vantage point, of the 20,000 places available in the country's high school system at Independence in 1962, back then only 11% (2,200) of all eligible school-age students could gain access to secondary education.

THE STORY OF CAMPERDOWN HIGH SCHOOL

Manley had long felt that an expansion of educational opportunities was the key to the further development and growth of the country. A highly-regarded lawyer of international repute, Rhodes Scholar, and outstanding high school athlete, Manley held the strong view that government could use its immense power as a lubricant to uplift the common people. In the general elections held in 1955, Manley's People's National Party's major campaign message depicted him as "the man with the plan." Manley believed in the power of education as a major driver in a people's future.

When Camperdown opened for the school year in September 1958, the influx of new students increased the student population to 330. At the same time, decisions had to be made with respect to the old facilities at Portland Road. Acting on the suggestion of Reverend Miller, it was determined that the school would continue to offer evening classes, maintaining a tradition started in the 1930s. This morphed into the Extension School at Portland Road, which was formalized and expanded to operate as a co-ed institution to accommodate as much as 300 students. By 1964, operations were moved to the Camperdown Road campus in order to accommodate the growing number of students then seeking the opportunity for secondary learning, but not succeeding in the examination to gain entry into the high schools. At the end of the first term, 84 students were on roll in the Extension School.

It was agreed that the Extension School would operate under the guidance of the Principal of the Day School, but would, in essence, operate as a stand-alone facility with its own Dean and Director of Studies, Head Girl and Head Boy and Prefect body. For girls in the Extension School, the first uniform was all-white – white skirt and white blouse; for boys it was khaki. School hours would run from 2 pm to 6 pm, Monday to Friday. Hours for the Day School – 8 am to 2 pm, Monday to Friday, with a short lunch break. The uniform for the Day School remained the same as before for the girls—brown tunic with white blouse—and khaki for the boys, with brown and white epaulettes.

According to Dr. Hazel Linton, who attended the Extension School between 1963 to 1965, and served as Head Girl (1964-65), the uniform for

MAJOR BUILDING YEARS: 1960s – 1970s

the girls in the Extension School was changed (circa 1963) to the same plaid used in the Day School. For the boys, the khaki uniform would remain as before, but for the girls, it would be white blouse, a skirt of the same plaid material used by the Day School, with a tie of the same plaid, and a straw hat with a plaid band. Teachers for the Extension School were drawn from the Day School and from other high schools. Dr. Linton recalls that Professor Harriott, a teacher in the Day School, also taught Health Science in the Extension School. She also remembers that Mr. Marcus Garvey, son of the National Hero and a teacher in another high school, taught Mathematics in the Extension School on a part-time basis.

Given the predominance of girls in the student population in the Day School, the administration settled on a two-to-one ratio of girls to boys. That September (1958) and the following January (1959) saw a few "older" boys (12+) entering the school, most coming through the Common Entrance Examination route.

One of the boys in the new cohort, Everald Fletcher, who attended Camperdown from 1959-63, reminisced about his feelings after being placed in this previously all-girls' high school. His first choice for a high school was Kingston College, his neighbourhood high school. Fletcher, in any event, won the 2nd prize for his new school in the All-Schools singing competition in the U-14 Boys Soprano category.

He reminisced on his Camperdown experience:

> I remember seeing the brown and white uniform but I knew very little about Camperdown. When I visited Camperdown, my first thought was that it did not appear to be a school. It reminded me of a great house with approximately eight or nine large rooms and two floors. Several feet away, detached were two rooms used as class rooms, attached to a gazebo-type area, where we assembled each morning before classes began. At the other end of the gazebo were two other class rooms....
>
> My first day at Camperdown still leaves a vivid picture in my mind. My well laundered khaki suit, being worn for the first time... the shirt my mother made, with the brown and white school epaulettes. My shiny black shoes. My well-groomed hair. I felt so proud!

I was placed in Form 2B with 33 other students, 16 girls and 18 boys. I sat with great trepidation as Miss Panton our form teacher discussed the curriculum for the first semester. There were new subjects such as Latin, Spanish, Algebra and Geometry. I felt quite overwhelmed.

The ringing of the third-period bell signaled that it was time for a break. We gathered around the only water fountain, which had 6 to 8 faucets. Actually getting to one of these faucets from the first day proved to be a challenge. I later realized that the total number of students in attendance was 300….

At lunchtime, we ate in our classrooms. You either brought your lunch or it could be bought at the tuck shop. I observed that the school had predominantly girls in the upper classes.

The Principal, Mr. White, was a workaholic. He was involved in all aspects of the school. His involvement included but was not limited to being the Athletic Coach. He worked alongside the Groundsman/Caretaker, removing debris and assisted in maintaining a clean, obstacle-free playground.

Mr. White would spend very little time in the office. He conducted the morning worship, in the afternoons he would be observing Drama and Singing, also sports such as Softball, Netball, Cricket, Soccer (Football)). He coached Track and Field.

My co-ed experience prepared me for life. I made many lasting friendships. I am particularly proud of many of my fellow students. They have excelled in sports, entertainment, politics, journalism, education, and academics.

For such a small school, we have made a great impact in Jamaica and around the world.

***

January **1959**: But Camperdown's previous status as a private school also did not sit well with many of the girls assigned by examination to this high school. Here's what Mrs. Lois Anderson (then Lois Stewart) remembers from her time at Camperdown as a precocious 12-year old:

MAJOR BUILDING YEARS: 1960s – 1970s

Imagine my apprehension on that Monday morning in January 1959 when I entered the gate at 6B Camperdown Road. I was wearing my cocoa-brown tunic, white blouse, cocoa-brown beret, brown lace-up shoes and brown socks. Of course, I cannot forget my brown grip that served as both my book bag and lunchbox. I was sent to an outdoor classroom with approximately 4 rows of connected desks and benches. Oh…my class was 2B. There were about 30 students; lucky for me I knew 2 of my classmates, Bobby Aquart and Sammy Burke (he was in 2A). All of the other kids were strangers to me. I had to get used to being called "Lois," which is my first name. However, I had not used that name in years because it was always mispronounced. I had preferred to use Beverley, which is my middle name, but could not because there were already 3 other Beverleys in my class. So, I settled for Lois.

Soon after I arrived that day, I requested a transfer to another school but the Headmaster, Mr. Noel White, refused to approve it. During the 5 years I spent within the walls of Camperdown I grew to love it and, after another 50-plus years since graduation, I still hold wonderful memories and lasting friendships..

To get the "new" Camperdown going, a number of changes were set in place. Mrs. Ivy Grant, founder and Headmistress since the school's founding in 1930, was given a two-year leave of absence to complete a university degree, in keeping with the policy that grant-aided high schools be headed by someone with a degree. New graduate teachers also had to be recruited to bolster the teaching staff carried over from the old school. Previously, most of the teachers held teaching certificates from teacher-training colleges; this would now need bolstering with university graduates. It is interesting to note that in a survey taken in 1943 of the island's secondary school teachers, only twelve percent were trained graduates, while less than 22 percent held qualifications above the Senior Cambridge School Certificate.

The curriculum continued to provide for instruction in English Language and Literature, Religious Knowledge, Jamaican and West Indian

History, Geography, Mathematics, Latin, Spanish, Biology, Health Science, Art, Commercial subjects, Needlework, Singing and Elocution, and Physical Education. Other activities included track athletics, cricket, football, volleyball, netball and softball. There were also activities in Drama, Inter-Schools Christian Fellowship, a Guide Company, the Historical Society, the Debating Society and the 4-H Club. Students were prepared for the Senior Cambridge School Certificate examination, the Higher School Certificate examination, the General Certificate of Education (Ordinary Level), the examinations of the Royal Drawing Society, as well as to reach proficiency in commercial subjects.

Among the new teachers holding university degrees recruited to boost the school's faculty was Mr. Keith King, a Barbadian graduate of the local university who taught English, English Literature, and Latin, as well as serving as Sports Master. Miss Winifred Crooks taught English and English Literature to the upper forms. Miss Pearline Panton taught Geography and also served as Games Mistress. Reverend Gladstone Donalds, School Chaplain, also taught Religious Knowledge. Reverend Donalds was the first coloured Minister to head the St. Paul's Presbyterian Church on Lockett Avenue. But even as the school progressed, the facility for the teaching of science was non-existent. Professor Oscar Harriott, who held undergraduate and graduate degrees from the University of Nebraska in the United States, taught Health Science and Biology, doing so without the aid of a laboratory.

In a major effort to bolster the curriculum, additional graduate teachers were recruited over the next few years and included Miss Veta Manderson-Jones (West Indian History), Mr. Franz Botek (Chemistry), Miss Lydia Graham (Mathematics), Mrs. Claire Johnson (Science), Mr. Herbert Murdock (Spanish and Literature), Mrs. Pamela Mordecai (English and English Literature), and Mr. George Aboud (Chemistry—Lower School). In 1961, Mr. John Morgan was recruited from England to serve as Mathematics Master. In addition to his teaching duties, he also took on the task of leadership of the Cadet Corps. The early years also saw teachers as Mr. Philip Hamilton and Mrs. Rhoda Chambers.

Botek taught Chemistry in the upper school. Only four boys responded – Basil Bryan, Winston Buckley, Hubert Hicks and Leigh Ruddock. Classes were taught in the open yard, in the shade "under the mango tree." For the necessary lab work, the boys travelled two times per week to Kingston College, to work

MAJOR BUILDING YEARS: 1960s – 1970s

under the tutelage of Chemistry teacher, Mr. Joseph Earle, who later served as Principal of Jose Marti Technical High School and Calabar High School.

Many of the stalwart teachers from the "old" Camperdown (the non-University graduates) were retained: Mrs. Myrtle Burke; Mrs. Viola Aitcheson; Mrs. Ruby McFarlane; Mrs. Girvan; Mrs. Nora Malcolm: Mrs. Alda McCatty; Mrs. Melvie Reid, a remarkable teacher of Drama; Mrs. Isobel MacPherson; Miss Grace Sinclair; and Mrs. Carmen Barrow. Another of the "earlier" teachers retained was Mr. Raphael Forbes, holder of the Inter-B.A. degree, then working on attaining his full B.A. degree from London University. Mrs. G. Lindo was also retained to teach Art and Miss Dorrit Hoilett to teach Needlework. Dance would remain under the guidance of Miss Inez Green.

The early years were especially difficult ones calling for much sacrifice. It is to the tribute of these pioneering teachers of the "new" Camperdown, who stayed the course, not only out of loyalty to Ivy Grant, but moreso out of love for the fledging institution and their profound belief that the building of a better Jamaica would come only through education. They approached their work with a togetherness that happens only in a close-knit family with a fixity of purpose. One of these teachers remembers that in the old wooden building that housed the Principal's office, classrooms, staff room and sick room, "the senior staff would be sitting on chairs around a small table, while the junior staff would take their turn sitting on a day bed."

The person chosen to act in Mrs. Grant's absence was Mr. Noel White. He was initially assisted by 14 full-time and four part-time members of staff. White was to guide Camperdown through its first two years as a Grant-Aided school (1958 – 1960).

Noel Austin White came with impressive credentials. He previously served on the teaching staff of Jamaica College, Kingston College, and Calabar High School (where he was also Sports Master), and was highly regarded as one of the best history teachers in the country. White held a B.A. degree from London University, the Diploma in Education from the University of the West Indies, the Certificate in Education from Leeds University, and the M.A. degree from Columbia University. He took a keen interest in sports and ran a successful programme at Hotspur Track Club, which he founded in 1961. At Hotspur, he developed several of Jamaica's leading female sprinters, including Una Morris, who, at age sixteen, placed fourth in the 200 meters at the 1964 Olympic Games in Tokyo, Japan. He was Assistant Coach to the Jamaica team at the Central American and Caribbean Games in 1962 and the Tokyo Olympics in 1964. White also served on a number of church committees.

White immediately set about to raise Camperdown's profile in academics and sports, as well as to introduce significant other innovations. He was a man in a hurry. In order to accomplish his goal, he used his Principal's discretion to accept a few older boys on transfer from other high schools or other students (not necessarily those from any high schools, but) who were nonetheless successful in the Jamaica Local First and Second Year Examinations.

While the school was well regarded in girls' sports, particularly in softball and track and field, the situation with the boys was different. And so White plunged headlong into getting the school accepted into the annual Inter-Secondary Schools Sports Association's (ISSA) Track and Field Championships (Champs) for boys.

White's remarkable contribution to the school was publicly recognized when he was inducted, as a member of the inaugural class, into the Camperdown Hall of Fame in 2011.

In **1960**, there are 351 students enrolled (77 Government scholarship holders, 267 Government-aided students, 7 full fee-paying students). 28 students are entered by the school to sit the Senior Cambridge School Certificate examination—24 girls and four boys. Sixteen of the candidates are successful.

Groundbreaking takes place in January for the new building to be built by the Ministry of Education.

It was under White's leadership that Camperdown first entered Boys' Champs in 1960. Since the school had just started enrolling older boys, the entries were concentrated in Classes 2 and 3. Only three athletes were entered in Class 1 – Willard Edman (Head Boy – 1961), Winston Buckley and Hubert Hicks. In Class 2 there were Derrick Williams, Leopold Montieth, and Clive Brown. A team was entered in the Class 3 6x110-yard relay.

MAJOR BUILDING YEARS: 1960s – 1970s

White's hard work brought immediate success: Norman McKenzie, who was trained by White at the school's very small playground, took second place in the Class 2 120-yard hurdles. White also held some training sessions at the Police Training School ground on Elletson Road to overcome the deficits encountered at the school grounds. McKenzie was also the 4th place winner in the Class 2 High Jump to become the first Camperdown boy to win points at Champs. In order to overcome the lack of facility and equipment and the many different obstacles that had to be cleared, White employed a number of novel experiments to achieve his purpose, including McKenzie's running over the hurdles, while using a younger boy to sprint alongside to give McKenzie added incentive to run faster.

In this its first year at Boys' Champs in 1960, of the 21 schools entered, Camperdown wore number 20 (the next available number after all the schools that participated at the previous year's championships). This was the 50th year of the staging of the Championships.

McKenzie's four points elevated Camperdown to a 13th place finish, tied with Titchfield High School. Camperdown would thus wear number 13 the following year (1961).

The sports programme included, for boys: athletics, cricket and football, and for girls: athletics, netball and softball. In 1961, the school entered the 2nd Eleven cricket and football competitions among grant-aided schools. Basil Bryan (Head Boy—1962) was appointed captain for both cricket and football teams. Given the few "big" boys in the school, many had to participate in both sports. Among them were Sydney Marsh, Boris Gordon (later Boris Robinson), Hugh Gilchrist, Lascelles Williamson, Norman McKenzie, and Lennox Aquart. Some boys participated only in one sport, a few merely making up the requisite eleven players needed to field a team. The Colts football competition was also entered. Camperdown played several matches in cricket and football against 2nd Eleven teams from the other grant-aided schools, including Kingston College, Calabar, Jamaica College, St. Jago, Kingston Technical, Excelsior and Wolmer's. With Kingston College there was a special relationship based on the closeness between the two schools developed out of Noel White's tenure at Kingston College.

For girls, the Netball competition was entered for the first time and the response for participation was outstanding. Previously, Camperdown would entertain other schools in Netball, but only on a friendly basis. Numbered among the "bigger" girls, on whose shoulders rested Camperdown's competitiveness, were Joan Alcock, Beverly Brown, Lorna Brown, Yvonne Brown, Claire Forrester, Norma Lubsey, Carmen Ottey, Jean Pinnock (Head Girl, 1963-64), Sandra Pinnock, Norma Reid, Ethlyn Smith, Hermine Taylor, and Fay Wilson.

Camperdown continued active involvement in the Softball League and Violetta Thompson, affectionately called "Dream," was outstanding in this sport. The name "Dream," so the story goes, was attached to her given her smooth and brilliant playing. Thompson went on the represent Jamaica in Softball, and also played a leading role in Softball administration on the national scene.

In addition to sports, students remained committed to their involvement in Drama as well as in the annual Speech Festival. The Girls' Choir presented an Easter Service at St. Andrew Scots Kirk Church on Duke Street, and a programme of carols at the Jamaica Broadcasting Corporation (JBC). The Camperdown Choir also joined with the choirs from the other schools under the auspices of the Presbyterian Church (Meadowbrook, Iona, and St. Andrew) in performance at the General Assembly of the church's Synod.

Camperdown students continued to volunteer with the Save the Children's Fund and the Young Women Christian Association (the YWCA). During the year, educational trips were made by the History Society to Rockfort Mineral Bath, Port Royal, Spanish Town, the United Estates Factory at Bybrook, the Jamaica Alumina Works at Ewarton, Dunn's River Falls, to the Green Grotto caves, Cinchona Park, and, in collaboration with the Past Students Association, a weekend hike to the Blue Mountain peak.

1961: Ivy Grant returns to Camperdown in January 1961, just in time to welcome the newly constructed three-story building, equipped with six classrooms and two science laboratories for chemistry and biology courses. Construction started in January 1960, built at a cost of twenty-one thousand pounds. It is the first of a three-part programme for buildings at the school.

It is of note that for the first 31 years of its existence, Camperdown lacked an auditorium, a cafeteria, a proper laboratory, and had no playing field to speak of.

MAJOR BUILDING YEARS: 1960s – 1970s

Given the problems encountered with finding adequate space for the 341 students on roll, even before the formal opening, the classrooms in the new building were immediately pressed into use. It was in those classrooms that that year's Senior Cambridge Examination was administered to Camperdown students. The new building was officially opened in January 1962 by the Minister of Education, Honourable Florizel Glasspole, whose long-time association and keen support in the development of the school made it, according to him, an especially "historical occasion." The building was dedicated by Reverend Clement Thomas, Moderator of the Presbyterian Chuch. To further help with the crushing space problem, property adjacent to the school was also bought and the house on the premises used for additional classrooms.

By 1961, a new school board is in place. The principal change in its composition was Reverend Miller stepping down to serve as Vice Chairman, and the previous Vice Chairman, Mr. F.L. Sangster, now assuming the role of Chairman.

Ferdinand Llewellyn Sangster, the new chairman, was dedicated to the building of Camperdown. Much of the school's foundation in the early years depended on his support and deep involvement.

Sangster was an eminent businessman in the field of commerce, rising to become the Managing Director of Sangster's Bookstores and senior partner in Collins and Sangster's, one of the largest publishing houses in the Caribbean. Remarkably, for a person of his stature in the business world, he was a practicing Christian and a dedicated servant of the church. He served on various church committees, as Chairman of the Finance Committee and Treasurer for many years; and as a member of the Board of Elders at Lincoln Kirk and Hope United Presbyterian Church.

As Chairman of the School Board from 1961-1974, Sangster was a generous benefactor and made many personal sacrifices to help Mrs. Grant build Camperdown. Part of the land that the school occupies was acquired through his own expense.

In a moving tribute paid to Sangster by the Church Synod in 1977, it was noted that "the present structure of Camperdown High School stands as a monument to [his] leadership of the Board of Governors of that school."

∽∂∾

The successful results of the Senior Cambridge School Certificate examination for 1960 emboldened the school to establish its first Sixth Form class by January 1961. The class comprised six students: four girls – Sylvia Anderson (Rennalls), (Head Girl – 1961), Monica Givans, Aileen Gooden, Hyacinth Terrelonge, and two boys – Louis Lindsay and Willard Edman.

1961 examination results are even more impressive. Thirty-seven students sit the Senior Cambridge School Certificate examination and eight sit the GCE (General Certificate of Education). Twenty of the 37 are successful – one earning Grade I, and three earning Grade II. Norma Reid is the top performing girl and Basil Bryan the top boy.

Based on the improved results in Needlework from the year before, more girls are attracted to offer it as a subject. The Parent-Teachers Association, encouraged by the results, donates two new sewing machines to the school. The Parent-Teachers Association also collaborated with the Past Students Association to host a fair to raise funds for further development. The fair was opened by Lady Allan; student Alice Collins got the first prize in the Fashion Parade, with Jean Pinnock the first runner up.

In the Jamaica Secondary Schools Drama Festival, the school's drama group, under the leadership of tutor, Mrs. Melvie Reid, earned commendation for its presentation of "A Square Peg."

In 1961, the Camperdown Cadet Corps and the Camperdown Scout Troop, under teachers John Morgan and Raphael Forbes, are formed. Among the first students to participate are Hubert Hicks, Norman McKenzie, Everald Fletcher, Dennis Dixon, Dunston Wright, and Patrick Payne. Hicks and McKenzie would go on to become the first two student-officers in the corps.

In athletics, the girls continue to impress at the Inter-Secondary Schoolgirls Track and Field Championships (Girls' Champs). After a three-year absence, Girls' Champs returns to Sabina Park. At the 1961 renewal, Carol Pinnock wins the gold medal in the Class 2 Long Jump with a leap of 15 feet, 2-1/2 inches. In Class 1, Ethlyn Smith stuns everyone with the

MAJOR BUILDING YEARS: 1960s – 1970s

performance of the meet in winning the 80-metre hurdles in a time of 12.8 seconds, breaking the West Indies Championship record of 13.0 seconds. Hyacinth Hawthorne takes 4th place in the Class 2 80-metre hurdles, and Camperdown also wins the 6x80-yard Shuttle Medley event in a time of 1:2.2 seconds.

Accompanied with a picture of Smith gliding over the hurdles is the major headline of ***The Daily Gleaner***'s sport page (May 27, 1961): "CAMPERDOWN GIRL BREAKS W.I. RECORD." Smith is described by ***SportsLife*** magazine as "the best woman hurdler in the West Indies."

Camperdown ends Girls' Champs in 3rd place with 16 points, tied with Clarendon College.

In December, the school bids farewell to one of its longest-serving teachers as Mrs. Nora Malcolm retires. A luncheon in her honour is hosted by the Past Students Association at the Flamingo Hotel in Cross Roads and the guest speaker is the Honourable Florizel Glasspole, Minister of Education, who hails her as one "who did so much to build a better [Camperdown]."

During the year, Camperdown students are in the forefront of a drive to raise funds to support hurricane victims in British Honduras.

By the end of 1961, the staff component is 16 full-time and 5 part-time, while the school's enrollment increases to 358 students – 236 girls and 122 boys – including 77 Government scholarship holders and 267 grant-aided students.

1962: The students now number 341 – 228 girls and 113 boys, a continuation of the 2:1 ratio. As compared to the year before, the lower total reflects a new and growing situation in the country as many young people, including students, leave via migration to join parents in England and in the United States. Over the course of a few years, several students leave, such as Hector Alfonso, Charlie Tatum, Canute Feurtado, and Barrington Taylor. Tatum and Taylor are quickly drafted into military service. Tatum, who serves 30 months in Vietnam, marries a Vietnamese woman and returns to the United States. One of his three sons from this marriage, Mark Tatum, goes on to become the Deputy Commissioner of the National Basketball Association.

Cambridge School Certificate examination results show 64% passes in all subjects, with eight students attaining Grade 2. In English, 40 of 41 students are successful, while in History 46 of 48 are successful, with four distinctions and 33 credits.

THE STORY OF CAMPERDOWN HIGH SCHOOL

The first group of students sits the Cambridge University (Overseas) Higher School Certificate examination, and Louis Lindsay becomes the first Camperdown student to be successful at this level.

In the Jamaica Secondary Schools Drama Festival held at the Little Theatre, Camperdown's entry is "Farewell King," a Shakespearean play based on the life of King Richard II. Derrick Williams (Head Boy – 1963-64), Sylvia Anderson, and Lascelles Williamson give excellent performances and receive rave reviews. Derrick Williams continues his outstanding performances and wins first prize in Boys' Class II Verse Speaking at the All-Island Speech Festival, an event sponsored by the Poetry League of Jamaica and the Jamaica Festival of Arts Committee. After leaving Camperdown, he becomes one of the country's leading dancers, before moving on to an impressive international dancing career.

The school is also involved in an Exhibition presented by the History Teachers Association at the Institute of Jamaica that highlights "pages of Jamaica's history." Camperdown's exhibition covers "The House of Assembly: 1800-1884" and reflected models, paintings, drawings, maps, and charts of the period.

In the Civics competition sponsored by the Citizen's Committee for a Better Jamaica, Norman McKenzie is awarded a first prize; Alexandrine Hobson takes first prize and the Moderator's Cup in the Harmony in the Homes essay competition. The Girl Guides, under the leadership of past student, Fidelia Johnson, take part in the Youth Rally at the country's Independence Celebrations in 1962. The Camperdown Choir, under the inspiration of Tutor, Mrs. Ruby McFarlane, is invited by Mr. Lloyd Hall, the Music Education Officer in the Ministry of Education, to perform at various Independence events throughout the island.

During the year, past student Basil Bryan wins selection from the Cable & Wireless company to attend its West Indies Training School in Barbados to pursue a 1-year course in Telecommunications. He finishes the course in 7 months (the first and only student to achieve this) and returns to Jamaica to join the staff of the company.

On October 15, 1962, the school receives its first Government inspection as a grant-aided school.

Extra-curricular activities are in full mode as the school's choir makes a presentation at the Presbyterian Church's Synodical Young People's Missionary service at St. Andrew Scots Kirk Church.

MAJOR BUILDING YEARS: 1960s – 1970s

1963: The school continues to grow in both students and staffing. The staff provide loyal and devoted service in the classroom and in all other areas of school life. To expand its physical space, the Board purchases some adjacent properties. A "Community Day" is organized to showcase the school and to promote it as a community school that parents should consider for their children. The church also grants a request of the school to send two Ministers to teach Scripture.

There is a change in the school year from one based on the calendar year (January – December) to one that runs from September to July. As a result of this change, some students spend an extra five-to-six months in the same form, politely called 1A Transits. There is also a change in the school uniform. The cocoa-brown and white uniform is replaced with the plaid tunic with white blouse, and straw hat with a plaid band. In the words of past student, Grace Strachan (Head Girl – 1966-67), "the uniform was changed from that very somber and dark brown to the lighter, more cheerful check pattern…." The boys would continue to wear the khaki uniform.

1963 is also the year that the General Certificate of Education (GCE—Advanced and Ordinary levels, offered by the University of London), replaces the Cambridge School Certificate and the Higher School Certificate examinations.

Students: 368 students are now enrolled – 223 girls and 145 boys, with 18 full-time and 7 part-time teachers. There are 28 students in 6th Form, including six students who transfer from Merl Grove High School. All students have at least one period of Scripture per week (in addition to morning worship). Some students offer Scripture as a subject in examinations.

The school participates in the Science Exhibition organized by the Association of Science Teachers of Jamaica and presents a chemistry display on "Fractional Distillation." Camperdown's essay in the Harmony in the Homes Bishop's Cup inter-schools "Family Life" competition is one of twenty-one submissions from other high schools to be retained in the West India Reference Library.

Camperdown is also one of 7 high schools (out of 19 grant-aided schools) invited to submit entries to participate in the second annual Anchor School Embroidery Contest, sponsored by the T. Geddes Grant Company.

Choir: The choir sings at the United Nations Flag-Raising Ceremony and assists the St. Andrew Singers in the St. Cecilia Day programme at St. Andrew Scots Kirk Church. They also take part in the broadcasting of Christmas carols.

Camperdown participates in the Jamaica Secondary Schools Drama Festival at the Little Theatre. Its entry is "The Curate in Charge."

Athletics: Llewellyn Facey scores Camperdown's only point at Boys' Champs with a 4th place finish in the Class II Long Jump. Facey is one of the many multi-talented athletes to attend Camperdown, representing the school in track and field, cricket, and football. He was also a member of the choir and the elocution group and served as Head Boy during 1965.

Softball: The school continues its prominence in the Secondary Schoolgirls Softball League under coach Roy Archer, assisted by teacher George Aboud. Matches are held at the General Penitentiary Staff Club field (Prison Oval) on Tower Street. Several of the girls also play in the adult senior league representing Greenwich Cubs, a team also coached by Archer.

The Camperdown Old Students Association enters the Women's Senior League Volleyball competition.

1964: In an expansion mode, the Board purchases three adjacent properties to extend the school's boundaries in an effort to increase classrooms and to add a cultural centre. A new block of classrooms is also promised by the Ministry of Education to improve teaching in Home Economics and Woodwork.

During the year, an educational survey of five Presbyterian schools (St. Andrew High School, Knox College, Meadowbrook High School, Iona High School, and Camperdown) is undertaken by a team of educators comprising local and overseas members.

By 1964, the Extension School is fully operational at the Camperdown Road campus of the Day School and enrollment is steadily increasing.

During this period, the Day School bids farewell to teacher Miss Pearline Panton, who was offered a Lyndon B. Johnson Scholarship at Boston University to pursue a nine-month course in Child Guidance and Counseling.

Jean Pinnock is a runner-up in the "Miss Sixth Form Association 1963" contest at the Annual Sixth Form Ball held at the Myrtle Bank Hotel. The contestants were judged on a basis of personality, deportment, intelligence, and dress. The contestants represented 11 grant-aided schools.

MAJOR BUILDING YEARS: 1960s – 1970s

The decision is taken to increase the school's presence in Inter-Scholastic sports. A three-man committee is formed with Mr. McD. Messam, a member of the school board, Keith King, Sportsmaster, and past student Basil Bryan. The immediate focus is on track and field and football. The lack of a field prohibited an emphasis on cricket at the time. While earlier arrangements are in place with the Kensington Cricket Club to use its facilities at Kensington Park, this proves somewhat problematic where cricket is concerned. The boys have use of the field at Kensington Park for only two hours per day, from two to four p.m., three days per week. This affects the playing of house and practice matches requiring more time to complete. New arrangements are thus made to use the grounds of the then-closed Wembley Club at Dunoon Park (now the location of Dunoon Technical High School).

Athletics: Mr. Messam is the coach. In Boys' Champs, Camperdown gains nine points, all in Class 2, with Llewellyn Facey contributing to all nine points. Facey is 3rd in both the 100 and 220 yards, and, with Barrington Taylor, is the dominant sprinter on the second-placed 4x100 yards relay team. The school places 11th at Champs with 9 points.

In Girls' Champs, Camperdown scores 8 points and is tied for 10th place with Queen's High School, St. Mary High School, and Vere Technical High School. Yvonne Mitchell is champion girl in Class 3 with 7 points (1st in the 80 yards: 2nd in the 100 yards). In Class 2, A. Simon takes 4th place in the 100 yards. The coach is past student Willard Edman.

Football: Camperdown enters the Manning Cup competition, along with another first-timer St. Andrew Technical High School, with the following results: Points earned – 4, with 2 wins and 8 losses. The team scores 10 goals in the season, while giving up 31 goals.

The coach is Jamaica player Lascelles Dunkley and the squad includes: Altamont Howell (Capt.), Hugh Gilchrist, Derrick Burton, Winston Hobson, Lennox "Bobby" Aquart, Llewellyn Facey, Vernon Edwards, Samuel "Sammy" Burke, Dennis Dixon, Michael Murray, Alfred "Teddy" DaCosta, Michael Larrow, Mervyn Coy, Barrington Taylor, Bab Clarke, Roland Anderson and Courtland Nelson. The focus is on speed, with several outstanding sprinters in the squad.

It should be noted that Camperdown first applied to enter the Manning

Cup in 1963. However, the Inter-Secondary Sports Association (ISSA) requested that the school hold off until 1964, as the association was dealing with some administrative issues that had to be resolved.

It is a tough welcome! In the first match, Camperdown loses to Kingston College by a score of 7-0. Other losses are to: Wolmer's 1-0; St. George's 6-1; Kingston Technical High School 4-2; Calabar 4-1; Jamaica College 1-0; St. Jago 3-1; St. Andrew Technical H.S. 3-1.

Camperdown wins two matches, beating Ardenne 3-2 (Camperdown's first Manning Cup victory), and Excelsior 1-0.

Camperdown's first goal in the Manning Cup competition is scored by Bobby Aquart against St. George's. Dennis Dixon is the team's leading goal-scorer for the season.

Despite ending the season with a 2-8 win/loss record, there are encouraging signs, especially as the young team would return most of the squad for the next season. In a ***SportsLife*** magazine (57th Edition, 1964) article on the Manning Cup season, noted sportswriter, Sydney "Foggy" Burrowes, referred to the team as "The Mystery Men," and wrote: "Camperdown was certainly the mystery team of the Manning Cup season. Individually, they were good and could certainly have finished among the top four. In Facey they had a player of All Manning calibre. But have there ever been so many selfish players on a team?…They need a tough and experienced coach who can make them pull together if they are to realise their considerable potential." Aquart was later described by Burrowes as the team's "only truly unselfish player."

The Technical Department is created to offer courses in Woodworking, Technology, Metallurgy, Electricity and Electronics and Technical Drawing at the CXC level. In the Harmony in the Homes essay-writing and poster competition for secondary schools, Arlene Harris wins the Rt. Rev. C.A. Thomas Cup.

1965: The number of students increases to 395 (244 girls and 151 boys) and the faculty is now comprised of the Headmistress and a staff of 20. Despite problems, the environment provided opportunities to be optimistic with an added emphasis on improving the academics. In the GCE "O" level examinations, 31 students are entered and 21 pass with three or more subjects. There are three passes at the Advanced Level.

The Extension School is under the leadership of Mr. W. A. Johnson, the

MAJOR BUILDING YEARS: 1960s – 1970s

Dean and Director of Studies. There are 80 students on roll. In June of that year, the first set of students are sent for the GCE.

Fourteen-year-old Jennifer Holder wins a 15-volume set of the Britannica Junior Encyclopedia for her winning entry, "What Makes Us Sleep," in **The Daily Gleaner's** "Tell Me Why" column.

In Champs, the girls finish in 9th place out of 23 schools entered (tied with St. Jago High School with 23 points). Roberta Thompson wins the Class 1 Long Jump and is 2nd in the 80-metre Hurdles. Thompson would later represent Jamaica in Softball. In Class 3 Jennifer Levy wins the Discus. The school is also 3rd in the 4x110y relay.

There is new buoyancy among the boys in preparations for the new track season. The much-improved results from the 1964 season and the higher-placed position at Champs accounted for this. There is also a sense of heightened expectation as the school, for the first time, enters a promising team in Class 1. Camperdown is one of the youngest schools in the Championships.

Sports day at Kensington Park comes with a great buzz, especially in anticipation of the Class 1 boys' 100 yards. Anthony Attride is without a doubt the fastest boy in this class, but at the end of the race the crowd is silenced when the results are announced: Bobby Aquart is the upset winner with Llewellyn Facey coming second, Barrington Taylor coming third, and Attride fourth. Great upset!

As a result of this order of placement, a confident air sweeps over the camp. The feeling spreads that the school is definitely in a position to be among the top teams in the Class 1 4x100 yards relay, usually a marquis event at Champs.

In Class 2, there is no doubt that Michael Murray would be among the top sprinters at Champs. In Class 3, much is expected from young sprinter Donald Quarrie.

Preparations at Wembley are under the direction of Coach Messam, assisted by Keith King and Basil Bryan.

Coach Henry Malcolm McDonald Messam, a quiet personality and a selfless member of the church and the school Board, was himself a top schoolboy sprinter. He was Head Boy and captain of the Calabar High School team that won Champs in 1936. His captaincy of the team was said to be a decisive factor in the team's victory.

Back in 1935, Messam, known as the "Midnight Express" for his sprinting prowess, won the 100 and 220 yards to carry Calabar to second place at Champs. Messam was later a member of Jamaica's team to the Central American and Caribbean Games in 1938, winning a medal as a member of the 4x100 yards relay team. With considerable generosity, he gave years of service to the church and to the building of Camperdown, in the process placing the school on the road to the well-earned reputation as the "Sprint Factory."

Preparation of the small squad takes place in an atmosphere of confidence, not to win Champs – that seemed rather unrealistic for such a small team – but to make a big impact. Much attention is given to the mental as well as the psychological aspects. A number of young boys, though not members of the track team, would be present at every training session – some were there merely to pass time, others to make any contribution asked of them, such as holding the finish-line tape, cleaning up, and other small tasks. It was one of those boys that Messam called upon to assist with record keeping and other incidental tasks, giving young Glen Mills his first involvement in organized athletics. Mills, 15 years old, performs well in his assignments and is "hooked." He goes on to further assist with the preparation and coaching of the school's track team, eventually taking over coaching duties, and rising to national and international fame as one of the world's great sprint coaches.

The team's uniform remained the same from earlier years – cocoa-brown silk shorts and white vest. The vest was the everyday men's merino. The shorts were made by the mother of one of the boys on the team. To boost the confidence and pride of the boys, preparations were made with a local tailor to build sweat pants from material bought from a local haberdashery, as it was difficult to obtain ready-made sweats in the school's brown and white colours. The thought that came to mind was that if the boys were expected to compete against better-resourced boys from the more elite schools, then they, too, must look the part.

The hard work paid great dividends and Camperdown began a long

MAJOR BUILDING YEARS: 1960s – 1970s

process in stamping its sprinting pedigree on Champs. The results over the next several decades speak to this extraordinary success.

In Class 1, Anthony Attride lived up to the school's expectation by placing second in the 100 yards, running 9.9 seconds to Lennox Miller's (K.C.) 9.8 seconds. Attride remembers that momentous day:

> When I lined up for the final, among the final six in the event, I reminded myself that I was well prepared for this occasion, that the many, many days of training were now behind me, that now 'push cum to shove.' I knew that I was ready, fully prepared to make my mark.

In the highly anticipated Class 1 4x110 yards relay Camperdown turned in a classy performance. Aquart led off with a powerful first leg; Facey did the backstretch; Taylor ran the third leg, and Attride carried the baton home to gain second place to Kingston College.

In Class 2, Michael Murray places 3rd in the 100 yards and 2nd in the 220 yards. Murray also takes the 120 yards hurdles in a record time of 14.4 secs. He wins the award as Champion Boy in Class 2 with nine points.

In Class 3, Donald Quarrie shatters the 100-yard record with a new time of 10.9 seconds in the heats. His victory in the final is so dominant, so overwhelming for someone at that age, that the Headmaster of the school with the previous record demanded to see his birth certificate to verify Quarrie's eligibility to run in Class 3.

It was a glorious end to Champs: the boys end with 21 points, in 5th place out of 30 schools entered.

Football: Camperdown enters the 1965 Manning Cup season with greater expectations, considering that most of the members from the 1964 team are returning. Surprisingly, Camperdown is picked by some, including sportswriter and enthusiast, Foggy Burrowes, as potentially the best team in the competition outside of Kingston College. The lack of a playground means that Wembley would again be used. Disappointingly, results are similar to last year's. Overall, they play ten matches, ending the season with seven losses, two draws and one victory, for a total of four points. The one victory is against St. Jago, 2 – 1; the draws are against Calabar, 0 – 0, and Jamaica College, 1 – 1. The biggest loss is to K.C., 9 – 0.

Two members of the team – Anthony Attride and Courtland Nelson – are suspended for "ungentlemanly conduct."

Due to his outstanding performance in the competition, Llewellyn Facey is invited by National Coach Jorge Penna to join an All-Youth squad in preparation for a tournament in Central America.

1966: Enrollment is at 395 – 244 girls and 151 boys. Examination results show 31 students entered, with 21 passing 3 or more subjects at Ordinary Level: there are 3 passes at Advanced Level.

A new building is constructed for Woodwork, Industrial Arts and Cooking.

In Champs, Messam is the coach as the boys place 4th out of 33 schools entered (37 points). In Class 1, Attride is 3rd in the 100 yards; Michael Murray wins the 120 yards hurdles in a new record of 14.8 seconds, the first athlete to win the event in his first year in Class 1 since Louis Knight of St. George's College in 1951. Camperdown takes the silver medal in the Class 1 4x110 yards relay. In Class 2, Donald Quarrie is 2nd in the 100 yards. Godfrey Murray wins the 120 yards hurdles and takes 3rd place in the 880 yards. Camperdown also takes 2nd place in the Class 2 4x110 yards relay.

The girls in turn end at 14th place (13 points) out of 25 schools.

In 1966, Camperdown becomes the third Jamaican high school (after Kingston College and Excelsior High School) to enter a team in the Penn Relays, the prestigious international track and field meet held by the University of Pennsylvania in Philadelphia in the United States. The team consists of Michael Murray, Llewellyn Facey, Barrington Taylor and Anthony Attride, with Donald Quarrie as reserve. It is a most auspicious start as they take second place behind the defending champion, Kingston College, in the 4x110y relay. It was the beginning of many years of dominant sprinting by Camperdown at the Penn Relays spectacle.

Three Camperdown students are selected as members of the Jamaica All-Schools Track and Field team to tour the Eastern Caribbean – Anthony Attride, Michael Murray and Donald Quarrie.

In the following years, the school continues to expand and improve in all

MAJOR BUILDING YEARS: 1960s – 1970s

areas, guided by the steady work of the Principal and teachers. The publicity gained from strong performances in academics, sports (especially in athletics), and in other extra-curricular areas, elevate the school in the consciousness of the wider public.

Football: There is no Manning Cup as the competition is suspended for the year.

1967: The curriculum continues to expand with the introduction of new subjects.

Student Sonia Anderson submits the winning essay in the "Harmony in the Homes" competition with her entry, "How Should a Man Be Equipped for Marriage."

Camperdown is selected as one of five schools (Alpha Academy, St. Hugh's High School, Calabar High School, and Priory) to teach the German language. Camperdown's offerings for the Advanced Level examination would now include: Mathematics, Chemistry, Economics, English Language and Literature, Biology, Geography and German.

The Reverend T.A. Grant from the Lincoln Kirk Church assumes the post of Acting Chaplain – an effort to maintain the link between the school and the church. A special "Camperdown Sunday" service would be held once each term.

Camperdown students, conducted by Mrs. Ruby McFarlane, perform at the "United Nations Day," held in honour of the 67 member-countries of the United Nations represented in Jamaica.

Student Dahlia Keating of the Extension School is declared the winner of a Britannica World Atlas.

Past student, Constance "Grace" Burgess (Hastings) is one of three young Jamaican females selected by the British Overseas Airways Corporation (BOAC) to undergo an 8-week course in London to train as a hostess for the airline.

The Camperdown Players, under the tutelage of teacher Melvie Reid, win several major awards. The school's play, "The Proposal," wins the acting award in the annual Schools Drama Festival, with leading actors Jennifer Cameron (Head Girl – 1967-68), Bosville Salmon (Head Boy – 1968-69 and 1969-70), and Beresford Forbes. The play also wins the award for general production. Their entry in the National Drama Festival Five competition,

"Impossible Situation," wins the silver medal. Praise Myers (Head Girl – 1969-70) also wins an award; Teacher/Producer Melvie Reid and student Jennifer Cameron both receive commendations. Myers also wins an award for her rendition of "Blue Mountain Stream." Valerie Bailey receives special commendation for acting.

Camperdown's Inter-School Christian Fellowship singing group is invited to perform at the "Youth for Christ" convention and other Christian rallies throughout the country.

Cricket: Camperdown enters the Sunlight Cup for the first time, bringing to twelve the number of schools in the competition. This is a competition for grant-aided high schools in the Corporate area and Spanish Town. For the first time, the competition is organized into zones. Camperdown is in Zone B with Kingston College, Wolmer's, Excelsior High School, Kingston Technical High School, and St. George's College.

Excitement overcomes the school as past student Hopeton Lewis' song, "Take It Easy," becomes a big hit and reaches the number one position on the country's popular music chart. The song is credited with creating the popular Jamaican "Rock Steady" dance move. Lewis also has another hit, "Sounds and Pressure," at number four on the charts. Lewis goes on to become one of the country's leading entertainers, and continues his career in New York as one of the top voices in Gospel music.

Lawn tennis and Basketball are added to the school's sporting activities.

Athletics: In Boys' Champs, the school continues to perform at a high level, placing 3rd, with outstanding performances by new athletes. In Class 1, Hugh Taffe (Head Boy—1966-67) places 3rd in the 220 yards and Derrick Burton is 4th in the High Jump. In Class 2, Donald Quarrie is hailed as "the star of the show" as he takes both the 100 and 220 yards in record times, with Godfrey Murray 2nd in both. Murray also wins the 120-yard hurdles, with Roland Anderson in 4th place. In the Class 2 4x110y relay, the team of Errol Dillon, Roland Anderson, Godfrey Murray, and Donald Quarrie runs 44.1 seconds in the heats to break the record. They win 3rd place in the final.

In Class 3, two new stars arise—Patrick Minzie and David Garel, who both excel in the 100 yards, the 80-yard hurdles, and the Long Jump. Garel equals the record in the hurdles, running 11.4 seconds.

Murray is Class 2 Champion Boy with 10 points: Garel scores 9 points to become Class 3 Champion Boy.

MAJOR BUILDING YEARS: 1960s – 1970s

Football: The Manning Cup is now organized into zones; Camperdown plays in Zone A and ends with 3 points—1 win, 3 losses and 1 draw.

Camperdown drops out of the Secondary Schools Softball League, along with Tutorial College and Buxton High School.

The teaching staff is now at 21, including the Principal; 14 hold degrees. There are six auxiliary staff members.

1968: Ivy Grant retires as Principal. The Camperdown family also bids farewell to Deputy Principal, Mr. Raphael Forbes, after many years of service as a teacher in both the Day and the Extension schools. Forbes served as Dean and Director of Studies in the Extension School between 1966-1968.

Enrollment is now 420 students in the Day School, with an additional 160 in the Extension School.

James Fitz-Henry Brown, popularly known as "Jeff," is selected to replace Grant and would serve as Principal of Camperdown from 1968-1982. He immediately sets about raising the profile of the school.

Brown comes to the post with a keen interest in education. A graduate of Mico College (now Mico University) and the University College of the West Indies (now University of the West Indies), he comes to Camperdown after years of service at different levels of the educational process – from primary to tertiary, including a stint at Calabar High School. He also completed additional post-graduate studies at the University of Manchester in England.

Brown comes from humble background and sees education as a key instrument of development and progress, for the individual as well as the larger society. He is well-regarded for his outlook on different aspects of national life, from sports to politics to academics. A committed educator and a defender of the youth, the poor and the disadvantaged, he sees sports as a vehicle to develop a new and more confident Jamaica. Brown served as President of the Inter-Secondary Schools Sports Association (ISSA) for several years and played a key role in the decision when Kingston College and Calabar High School were both banned from participation in Champs for 1982, after an ugly infringement involving both schools the previous year.

It was under Brown's leadership that Camperdown embarked on a golden run in sports and extra-curricular endeavours, during which time Camperdown finished second in the team standing at Champs on four occasions in the 1970s. During his tenure as Principal, Camperdown was consistently competitive in the School's Challenge Quiz, was several times crowned All-Island Netball champions, won the Tappin Cup Limited over cricket competition in 1978, won the Manning Cup and Olivier Shield in 1978 and 1979, and won the schoolboy football triple crown (Manning Cup, Olivier Shield, and Walker Cup) in 1982.

In remarks in 1975, Brown made known part of his view on life:

> Given the new awareness, enthusiasm and revolutionary zeal of our youth today, it is hoped that they, our younger brothers and sisters, will be imbued with the determination to channel these admirable qualities into such constructive efforts as will enhance their own personal character and advancement and at the same time lead more significantly to the greater self-reliance and development of our country. If this is attained, neither they as persons, nor the school, nor Jamaica can fail.

To bolster the curriculum, Chemistry is offered at Advanced level and the Business Education programme is strengthened with the addition of Commerce and Accounts. Physics is added to the list of subjects offered by the Science Department in 1969. At the time of its introduction there is no Physics laboratory in place; such a facility would not be in place until 1972. The introduction of "A" Level Physics and Chemistry opens new horizons as Camperdown students could now be prepared to pursue science and medicine at the tertiary level.

1968 is another break-out year as the Camperdown community celebrates the news that past student Louis Lindsay is offered a Yale University Falk Foundation Fellowship, one of only twelve such Fellowships given by the university and open to the 24 post-graduate students chosen to study at the university from throughout the world. To celebrate this success, the old students' association holds a cocktail reception in his honour at the Sheraton Hotel.

Student Winston McKoy (Private First Class) wins selection as an exchange cadet in the Foreign Exchange course.

MAJOR BUILDING YEARS: 1960s – 1970s

The choir performs in a special Easter Festival of Music, "Youth in Concert," at St. Andrew Scots Kirk Church.

The Reverend Talmadge C. Ebanks is transferred to the Lincoln Road Church and assigned as school Chaplain. To expand the boundaries of the school, No. 5 Portland Road is purchased at a cost of 8,300 pounds.

Athletics: There is a change in the track and field programme as Mr. Messam hands over coaching responsibilities to Mr. Harold Scott and past student, Dennis Dixon. Mills now becomes an "unofficial" coach to the Class 2 boys, who, led by a few among them, seek his guidance, enjoy his way of thinking outside the box, and prefer to train with him than with the rest of the team.

Donald Quarrie continues his extraordinary dominance in sprinting at Champs, first in Class 2, and now in Class 1. In this his first year in Class 1, the country is greeted with the headlines: "Quarrie breaks 100, 220 yards records" (***The Daily Gleaner***, April 5, 1968), reporting that the "record breaking performances by Camperdown's Donald Quarrie in the 100 and 220 yards Class 1, highlighted yesterday's opening of the 58th annual Inter-Secondary Schools Athletics Championships at the National Stadium." Quarrie's new record in the 100 yards is 9.7 seconds, breaking the old mark set by Dennis Johnson in 1958 and equaled by Lennox Miller 1965. In the heats of the 220 yards, Quarrie's time of 21.4 seconds breaks Louis Knight's record of 21.8 seconds set in 1953 and equaled by Miller in 1965. Quarrie is even more dominant in the final as he wins in a new record of 21.2 seconds, breaking his own record set in the heats.

Quarrie is the Champion Boy in Class 1; Camperdown ends the meet in 4th place.

Camperdown further underlines its pedigree in sprinting in the Class 1 4x110y relay when Winston Hobson (Head Boy – 1967-68), Hugh Taffe, Godfrey Murray, and Quarrie run 41.4 seconds to break the old record held by Excelsior High School, set the previous year. However, in the final they lose to Excelsior, who won in a slower time of 41.5s.

In the special 2-day International Relay Carnival sponsored by National Continental Foods at the National Stadium, Camperdown's 4x110y relay team runs 41.3 seconds with the same four students to break the Jamaica junior record and establish a new junior world record in the event. Camperdown also wins the 4x220y relay in 1:27.7 seconds.

Camperdown becomes the first Jamaican high school to participate in three relay events at the Penn Relays – 4x110, 4x220, and 4x440y. They place 3rd in the 4x110y due to poor baton changing. The team is Hobson, Taffe, Murray and Quarrie. The other members of the squad are Patrick Minzie and Rupert McCleary. The officials accompanying the team are Mr. F. L. Sangster (Chairman of the Board), Mr. McD. Messam (Board member), Mr. Harold Scott (Masseur), and Mr. Dennis Dixon (Coach.

Seventeen-year-old Donald Quarrie is selected to represent the country in the 1968 Olympics in Mexico. He is the 2nd fastest sprinter on the national team.

Football: Camperdown is 8th out of 12 teams in the Manning Cup competition, with 3 wins, 6 losses, 2 draws.

1969: Past student and former teacher, Mrs. Irene Walter, is appointed as the Assistant Registrar at the University of the West Indies.

Football—Thirteen schools are entered. Of the twelve matches played, Camperdown finishes in 8th place—three wins, six losses, three draws. The wins are against Meadowbrook 3 – 2; Calabar 2 – 0; and Ardenne 2 – 1.

Horace Rose, is selected to the All-Manning team, becoming the first player from Camperdown to win this honour.

Athletics: The school welcomes a new coach, Mr. Glen Hester.

Donald Quarrie continues his assault on Champs records as he wins the Class 1 100 yards in a new record of 9.5 seconds. Quarrie runs 21.2s in the semi-finals of the 220 yards, equaling the record he set the previous year. He is, however, scratched from the final due to a stomach complication.

Mills' supervision of the Class 2 boys bears fruit as Minzie takes 2nd place in both 100 and 220 yards in Class 2. There is more excitement as they also win the Class 2 4x110y relay. Camperdown again finishes Champs in 4th place.

At the Penn Relays, Camperdown's 4x110y relay squad comprises Donald Quarrie, Ashton Waite, Godfrey Murray, Edward Quarrie and Rodney Fitz-Gordon. They finish in 3rd place but is disqualified due to a lane violation. Donald Quarrie also takes place in a special 100y race.

Quarrie wins an athletic (track) scholarship to the University of Nebraska in the United States. He later transfers to the University of Southern California. Quarrie is the first student/athlete from Camperdown to win an athletic scholarship. By 1970, at the age of 19, Quarrie is ranked as the number one in the world in the 200 metres, and by 1975 he becomes the first non-American to win the United States Amateur Athletics Union 100m race in one hundred years.

Over subsequent years, many other Camperdown student/athletes have won athletic scholarships. Numbered among the many are Ashton Waite (Federal City College in Washington, D.C.), Rodney Fitz-Gordon and Hugh Taffe (Howard University), Godfrey Murray (University of Michigan), Leroy Reid, Andrew Smith, Ralston Wright, Carey Johnson, Raymond Stewart (Texas Christian University), Andria Lloyd (Eastern Oklahoma University and the University of Alabama). Revolie Campbell (Mount San Antonio Community College), Sharon Moffat, Audrey Llewellyn-Hunter (Alabama A & M Univesity), Lorlee Giscombe, Verone Webber (Grambling University), Ronetta Smith (Louisiana State University), Trevor Gilbert (Clemson University), Orion Nicely (McKendree College), and Kimour Bruce and Saibel Anderson (Lincoln University). Many other Camperdown students have won scholarships to colleges and universities in the United States.

1970: The school sees a steady growth in the student population. The teaching staff increases to 32 full-time members, plus 5 Visiting Staff, and an additional 3 on the non-teaching staff. There are 9 members of the domestic staff. Additionally, there are 37 Prefects (29 Senior Prefects—6th Formers, and 8 Sub-Prefects—5th Formers).

In the Secondary Schools Drama Festival, Bosville Salmon, Praise Myers, Karen Harrison, Marcia Smith, and Victoria Grant give outstanding performances in the school's entry, "A Prior Engagement." The play receives an award "for a smooth and colourful production."

Glen Mills is now the official coach of the Boys' track team, a position he will hold for the next 30 years, during which Camperdown becomes a mighty force in sprinting and cements its place as the "SPRINT FACTORY," in the process dominating the sprint events at Champs, the Penn Relays, and other major junior athletic meets.

Camperdown finishes Boys' Champs in 4th place; the girls end Champs in 9th place with 30 points.

Rodney Fitz-Gordon continues Camperdown's dominance in sprinting by winning both 100 and 220 yards in Class 1. Camperdown also wins the

Class 1 4x110y relay. Donovan Russell finishes 2nd in the 100 and 220 yards in Class 2.

Roland Anderson is "Sports Boy of the Year." He is captain of the football team and also represents the school in cricket, track and field, and table tennis. He is invited to train with the Jamaica U-19 squad in preparation for the regional youth cricket tournament.

Janet Stanford is "Sports Girl of the Year." An outstanding athlete, she represents the school in track and field and netball. She is also a national representative in track and field.

Football: Camperdown finishes in 5th place: 8 wins, 2 draws and 1 loss. Two Camperdown players, Errol Clarke and Basil Salmon, are selected to the All-Manning team.

Camperdown is overwhelmed with joy as Donald Quarrie wins three gold medals at the Commonwealth Games in Edinburgh – 100m, 200m and 4x100m relay.

Past student and former Head Girl, Grace Strachan, wins the Government Savings Bank Centenary Scholarship (in honour of the bank's 100th year of operation) to study economics at the University of the West Indies.

1971: A new 5-year development plan is unveiled with financing from the World Bank. The Rev. Lewis Davidson, former Principal of Knox College who now serves as the Presbyterian Church's Education Advisor, is selected to assist the Board in executing the plan.

To raise funds for the school, the Past Students Association holds a number of activities. A Barbeque Supper is held at the Police Officers Club.

In the Jamaica Secondary Schools Drama Festival, Camperdown's presentation, "The Curate in Charge," wins first place for best adaptation of a foreign play to a Jamaican setting. Fay Grey, one of the performers in the play, is awarded a two-year scholarship to the Jamaica School of Speech and Drama for her excellent performance. George Campbell receives "Commendation" in the Poster Competition.

Athletics: The races are now in metres and the school's dominance in sprinting is extended with Edward Quarrie, younger brother of Donald,

MAJOR BUILDING YEARS: 1960s – 1970s

winning the Class 1 200 metres in a new record. Eric Barrett, who transferred to Camperdown from St. George's College, takes 2nd place in the Class 1 100 metres (after setting a record of 10.6s in the heats). He anchors the Class 1 4x100m relay team (Edward Quarrie, Donovan Russell, Patrick Minzie, Eric Barrett) to victory in 42.5s, a new record.

In Class 2, Winston "Danny" Brown and Norman "Terston" Martin win gold and silver medals in the 100 metres, while Glenford Stanford wins the Long Jump. Dave Heaven wins the Class 2 Shot Put and Discus titles and is co-champion boy in Class 2.

Camperdown also wins the 4x400m relay in 3:21.2s (a new record) with a memorable anchor leg from Barrett, who takes the team (Everton Powell, Patrick Minzie, Florizel Dennis, Eric Barrett) from third to victory. Camperdown ends Boys' Champs in 3rd place; the girls finish at 20th place.

At the Penn Relays, the 4x100m relay team finishes in 2nd place with Edward Quarrie, Donovan Russell, Patrick Minzie, and Eric Barrett. They run the same time as the winner. The other members of the squad are Florizel Dennis and Everton Powell. The brilliant Barrett is one of three schoolboys selected to represent Jamaica at the Guadeloupe Games.

Camperdown (girls) is the All-Island Junior Netball Champions.

Football: Of 13 teams in the competition, Camperdown finishes in 4th position, with 5 wins, 3 losses and 4 draws. Colin Jennings is selected to the All-Manning team.

1972: There is a steady increase in the teaching staff in the Day School, and Headmaster Jeff Brown is assisted by 36 full-time teachers.

A new house – Sangster House (Colour – Green) is added to honour the monumental contributions to the development of the school by Mr. F. L. Sangster. The school now has four houses.

The block that houses the administration offices, staffrooms, and classes is replaced by a new structure. New facilities are constructed to house Metal Work, Electrical Installation, Ceramics and Craft. More adequate laboratories are also equipped and an All-Purpose building erected.

Academics continue to show improved results in GCE Advanced Level examinations, with thirteen students successful in Mathematics, Physics, Economics, Zoology, English, and Art. At the Ordinary Level, 36 students gained three or more subjects. In the Extension School, the results are encouraging: six students gain three or more passes.

The Extension School continues to grow and deliver for its students.

It remains a self-supporting part of the Camperdown family. It continues to have its own Principal, assisted by a Supervisor and the various subject teachers. It also retains its own Head Boy, Head Girl and Prefect body, and there is keen competition between the Day and Extension Schools in various subjects and activities, such as sports, Labour Day projects, Open Day and Career Week. The Extension School continues to fulfill its mission in providing secondary education for students who failed to qualify for entry to the Day School. Character development remains an important feature of the training so that graduates become better equipped for employment.

Students in the Extension School are prepared for a variety of examinations, such as the General Certificate of Education; the Royal Society of Arts in Principles of Accounts, English and Commerce; Pitmans – Book Keeping, English and Commerce; and the Jamaica Schools Certificate Examination.

In the Day School, students continued to be engaged and encouraged in expressing themselves on a variety of topics. One letter from a precocious student questions why African history was not taught in schools in Jamaica. "Let us admit," the letter-writer said, "that the vast majority of Jamaicans are of African descent."

A Library Club is formed to encourage students to read more widely and intelligently and to engage students in cultural and educational visits.

The school produces "Let Us Praise Him," a booklet of hymns intended to make student worship more inspiring and meaningful. Produced by members of staff and students in 4th, 5th, and 6th forms, the school tries to infuse new life in morning worship. In addition to the hymns and other praise songs, the booklet includes the Lord's Prayer, the National Pledge, and the National Anthem.

The school Orchestra is formed with past student, Angella Fortella, Secretary to the School's Bursar, as Pianist. Another past student, noted dancer Patsy Ricketts, is engaged to teach creative dancing.

Athletics: Under Coach Glen Mills the team continues to excel, placing 2nd at Champs, quite a remarkable achievement as the school has only 300 boys. The track team has only 30 athletes. Camperdown wins the Class 2 4x100m relay, as well as setting a new record of 3:19.1s in winning the Open 4x400m relay (Everton Powell, Patrick Minzie, Florizel Dennis, Eric Barrett), thanks to Barrett's brilliant anchor leg. Danny Brown is 2nd in the Class 1

MAJOR BUILDING YEARS: 1960s – 1970s

100m. Glenford Stanford takes the sprint double in Class 2 and also wins the Long Jump. Stanford is champion boy in Class 2.

Eric Barrett is now recognized as one of the future stars in Jamaica's track constellation. In 2016, at a special function to honour Mills, Barrett had this to say:

> Mr. Mills was my proper introduction to a coach, and it was baptism of fire, but one that was a blessing as his natural gift to unearth potential, and his distinct talent at molding had proved to be of immediate benefit not only to me but also the 30-plus young men making up the Camperdown track and field team which he oversaw that reaped record-breaking results at Boys Champs that year.

Barrett, also acknowledged as an "icon" at Champs, is described as one of the most outstanding sprinters in the history of Champs:

> He was a star on two high school track teams and broke several records – including one of the most prestigious sprint marks – at Boys' Champs, and was class champion on two separate occasions.... though he clearly belongs on the high school sprinting pantheon, [he] may not be as much of a household name as he should be.... Barrett truly belongs in the top echelon of Champs stars. He may simply have been born at the wrong time.

Football: The Manning Cup competition is suspended for the year.

1973: Camperdown leaves Boys' Champs as the 2nd place winner. In Class 1, Danny Brown is second in the 100m and 200m. Herbert Harris wins the Class 3 200m, is third in the 100m, and is the outstanding Class 3 athlete. Camperdown is also third in the Class 2 4x100m relay, and wins the Medley relay, thanks to an outstanding anchor leg by Anthony Hurbs. In Class 2, Errol Atland is second in the 800m, and third in the 400m.

Netball: In the 1972/73 season, Camperdown wins the Corporate Area Junior Cup, led by shooter Rosemarie Anderson. In the 1973/74 season, the school is the All-Island Senior Netball champion.

1974: In the Secondary Schools Drama Festival, Camperdown's entry "Odale's Choice" is well received. The play is under the direction of Mr. Keith Noel. Students Sharon Woolery, Pamela Cooper and Lewis Davis are outstanding in performance.

Camperdown finishes Boys' Champs in 2nd place. Sedley Webster wins the Class 2 400m and Trevor Bucknor wins the Class 2 High Jump and is 3rd in the Long Jump.

In Football, Phillip Davidson is selected to the All-Manning team.

1975: There are 26 successes in the Cambridge GCE "A" Level examinations. Camperdown's 5th and 6th formers stage an Arts & Craft Display at the Kingston & St. Andrew Library on Tom Redcam Avenue. The Parent Teachers Association of the Day and Extension schools hosts an "International Supper" at the school to raise funds to support the school. Camperdown students also stage an annual Pre-Christmas Variety Concert at the State Theatre in Cross Roads.

Athletics: Girls' Champs—Camperdown finishes in 5th place, after a 15th place finish the previous year. Coach Dorothy Hobson is assisted by Glen Mills and another past student, Wycliffe Robinson. Thanks to a superb 3rd leg by Verone Webber, Camperdown wins the Class 2 4x100m relay in a record time of 47.6secs. Top athletes are Lorlee Giscombe, Verone Webber and Sharon White. All three are chosen to represent Jamaica at the Freedom Games. Webber and Giscombe also represent Jamaica at the Carifta Games in Bermuda. Webber turns in a magnificent performance as she wins gold medals in the U-17 Girls 200m and 400m. She also captures the silver medal in the 100m.

Boys' Champs: the team finishes in 3rd place. Desmond Ricketts wins the Class 1 Long Jump title, while Sedley Webster is 2nd in Class 1 400m and 800m.

In the Gibson Relays, Camperdown wins the Herb McKenley Cup for its victory in the 4x400m relay.

Sedley Webster is selected as part of an 8-athlete team to represent Jamaica at the annual International High School Track and Field Championship in Chicago. Glen Mills is part of the coaching staff.

Netball: Led by star shooter, Rosemarie Anderson, Camperdown takes the double by winning the Corporate Area Netball title and the All-Island

MAJOR BUILDING YEARS: 1960s – 1970s

Senior Netball title. The other team members: Norma Ramsey (Captain), Minnette Edwards, Donnette Anderson, Sharon Lawrence, Sharon Moffatt, and Donna McCook. Cherita Robinson from the junior team is the reserve.

Throughout her scholastic career Rosemarie Anderson is a prolific goal-scorer. She is invited as a member of the national Colts and Junior teams.

By the early-1970s, Principal Jeff Brown decides to change the school's colours in sporting activities from cocoa-brown and white to Flame Red and Royal Blue. The move from brown and white to red and blue was taken in gradual steps. As the situation emerged, the school would use brown/white in track and field, but red/blue in football. Eric Barrett recalls that "I ran in brown and white and played Manning Cup in red and blue." The new colours chosen come about with the twinning of two house colours – Grant and Miller. The decision to do this comes after much difficulty in procuring brown and white football jerseys. After going through this in a gradual way, Camperdown would henceforth be identified by the dominant Flame Red and Royal Blue.

In 1975, Camperdown is a semi-finalist in the Walker Cup and loses 3-0 to Kingston College. Three members of the team are named to the 16-member All-Schools football team – Mark Salmon, Hugh Bailey and Desmond Ricketts.

Under Coach Carl Brown, who guided the football team from 1974-77, the 1976 and 1977 teams are considered to be among the best in the Manning Cup, but, unfortunately, do not meet with the expected success. Players on these squads include Anthony Lewis, Thomas McLean, Frank Sutherland, David Burgess, Donald Davidson, Hugh Bailey, Johnathon Palmer, Barrington Edwards, Hugh Bent, Patrick Dawes, Desmond Ricketts, Ripton White, Mark Salmon and Carlton Williams.

1976: The Reverend Raymond G. Coke is now in place as Chairman of the Board of Governors. The Minutes of the Eleventh Annual Synod of the United Church of Jamaica and Grand Cayman (March 8-11, 1976) recorded that Reverend Coke "was appointed Chairman in succession to Mrs. Gloria Levy who found it difficult to continue."

In the Secondary Schools Drama Festival, Winston Bell wins the "Best Actor Award."

In the Sunlight Cup cricket competition, Camperdown reaches the semi-final round but loses to Tivoli Gardens High School. The leading players are Trevor Chambers, Donald Morrison, Phillip Lawrence, Adrian Faulkner, and Earl Melbourne.

Boys' Champs: Camperdown finishes in 3rd place. Desmond Ricketts wins gold in Class 1 long Jump. He also wins gold in the Triple Jump. Peter Hibbert wins the Class 2 100m and 200m in record times. In the 200m, he runs 21.9 seconds to become the first Class 2 athlete to break the 22-second barrier. Sedley Webster (2nd) and Sylvester Smith (3rd) are among the first Jamaican schoolboys to break the four-minute mark in the 1500m.

Camperdown wins the Class 2 4x100m relay in a time of 42.9 secs.

Girls' Champs: Camperdown places 4th overall. In the Class 2 4x100m relay, they run 47.7 seconds, a time that is better than the winning time in Class 1. In Class 1, Sharon White is 2nd in the 100m and 3rd in the 200m. In Class 2, Verone Webber is 2nd in the 100m and 200m. She also wins the Open 400m in a record time of 54.5s, handing a rare defeat to Jacqueline Pusey in her Champs career. Lorlee Giscombe wins the Class 2 100m hurdles in a record time of 14.6s; Sharon Moffatt places 2nd after breaking the record in the heats.

At the Carifta Games in the Bahamas, Peter Hibbert wins gold medals in the U-17 Boys 100m and 200m. Verone Webber wins the silver medal in the U-20 Women 400m.

Football: Hugh Bailey is selected on the Jamaica Youth Football Team under Coach Winston Chung-Fah.

In the Olympic Games in Montreal, Canada, Donald Quarrie wins the gold medal in the 200m and takes the silver medal in the 100m, becoming the first Jamaican to win a gold medal in a sprint event at the Olympics. This is the first gold medal that the country is winning at the Olympics in 24 years (since 1952). During the decade, Quarrie establishes himself as one of the greatest sprinters of all times, becoming the first male athlete to win three consecutive 100/200m double at the Commonwealth Games in 1974 and 1978, in addition to his first 100/200m double in 1970.

The Past Students Association hosts a "Victory Dinner" at the Pegasus Hotel in honour of Quarrie's monumental achievement. Guest Speaker at the function, the Honourable Seymour Mullings, Minister of State in the

MAJOR BUILDING YEARS: 1960s – 1970s

Ministry of Youth and Community Development, lauds the school for "building up such a reputation in sports in such a short period despite the adverse conditions" (*The Daily Gleaner*, September 6, 1976).

1977: Home Economics is introduced in the syllabus as a subject in the CXC examination.

Mr. Lancelot Livingston joins the staff at the invitation of the Principal and sets about restructuring the Physical Education programme at the school, setting Camperdown on a glorious path in high school sports. In 2012, after 30-plus years at the school, he is recognized for his contributions to the development of sports at the institution.

Athletics: Girls' Champs: Class 1 – Verone Webber is 2nd in the 400m. In Class 2, Sharon Moffat wins the 100m hurdles. Audrey Llewellyn wins the High Jump and is 2nd in the Long Jump, while Barbara Gayle wins the Class 3 Long Jump.

Boys: Peter Hibbert wins the Class 2 100m and is 3rd in the 200m.

At the Carifta Games in Barbados, former Camperdown student, Emmett DeCambre, now finishing high school in New York, wins the U-17 Boys 100m in a new record time of 10.51 seconds, a mark that would stand for 24 years and not broken until 2000. He also wins gold in the 200m.

Verone Webber wins the bronze medal in the U-20 Women 400m.

Football: Four Camperdown players are named to the All-Manning squad: Carlton Williams, Donald Davidson, Hugh Bailey and David Burgess.

Camperdown is in the final of the Tappin Cup cricket competition and loses to Tivoli Gardens High School. Earl Melbourne, who also represents Melbourne Club in the Senior Cup competition, is named to the 13-player Youth Team to participate in the Benson and Hedges Youth Cricket competition.

The Camperdown Extension School is in the playoffs in the Independent Secondary Schools cricket competition for the Hendricks Cup.

The Donald Quarrie High School, situated in Harbour View, is named in honour of Donald Quarrie, who is also immortalized in Reggae songs of the period.

THE STORY OF CAMPERDOWN HIGH SCHOOL

1978: The introduction of "Free Education" in 1973 by the Government leads to a dramatic increase in the number of students entering the country's high schools. By 1978, Camperdown's student population is over 1,400 for the two shifts. There are 53 students in Sixth Form alone. To meet this increased demand, the teaching staff is now at 66 full-time members.

In order to cope with the explosion in students, back in 1974 a double shift system was introduced to alleviate problems of limited classroom space, inadequate facilities and insufficient equipment in the school system. The idea behind this was rather simple: two different sets of students would be able to use the same facilities. The shift system would last for well over a decade, when it was more-or-less phased out after encountering many problems. With deteriorating social and economic problems throughout the country, there is much concern about the lowering of standards in the moral, intellectual and spiritual fiber of the young people in the society. Years of lawlessness and the erosion of respect for authority and law and order now came full force.

The report to the Fourteenth Annual Synod of the United Church in Jamaica and Cayman Islands addressed this. By 1978, the Extension School at Camperdown is phased out and the students absorbed into the Day School and placed in the second shift. This leads to new concerns, particularly detrimental to those students in the second shift, as enummerated by the Synod:

1. There is less emphasis and opportunity for each student to participate in extra-curricular activities, whether academic or sports related;
2. There is less emphasis placed upon the student and less time is available for the total development of each student;
3. The student is denied the enriching experiences of a large and integrated student body;
4. There are physical dangers related to both shifts in terms of the early start and the late ending to each day. For example, students for the second shift who arrive early have to mill around in the schoolyard, sometimes leading to disciplinary problems.

The shift system was introduced nationally to accommodate more students using the physical facilities of the existing schools as the availability of space was a major problem in the education system. The morning shift ran

MAJOR BUILDING YEARS: 1960s – 1970s

from 7:15 a.m. to 12:30 p.m., a little over five hours. The afternoon shift ran from 12:45 p.m. to 5:30 p.m. To manage the two-shift system with the assimilation of the Extension School into the Day School, two Vice-Principals are named – Mrs. Winifred Smith and Mr. Stanley Williams—one for each shift.

Though there is some overlap, each shift carries its own teaching staff, including senior teachers. Problems arise in finding suitable teachers for each shift, essentially leading to overworked teachers and under-served students. The general unavailability of teachers throughout the education system grows worse each year that the shift system is in place.

As is the situation with other schools, Camperdown students now take the CXC examinations set by the Caribbean Examinations Council. Subjects include English, Mathematics, Geography, History, Accounts, Principles of Business, and Typing. Students continue to take A Level subjects in the GCE.

230 Fifth formers and 20 Sixth formers graduate. GCE results range from 71 percent passes in History, 52 percent in English Language, to 28 percent in Additional Mathematics. Good results are obtained in several other subjects.

Students now participate in a Careers' Week programme, directed at the middle and upper schools, and exposing Camperdown students to speakers in a wide range of career choices. There are also visits by students to various business establishments and organizations to further expose them to the world they will join.

In the Secondary Schools Annual Drama Festival, Camperdown garners excellent reviews. The plays presented in both 1977 and 1978 are written by student Seymour Taylor. The 1977 play, "Sandra," was also presented in the National Drama Festival in 1978, winning three awards: (1) Best Play by a local writer; (2) Best Musical; and (3) Best Produced and Directed play. Seymour Taylor and Sharon Woolery (HG – 1978-79) are the leading actors in the play. The J.A.L. Golding Cup for best director is awarded to Mr. Keith Noel, who directed "Sandra."

Noel Dwyer also wins an award for his performance in the play, "Legend of Asare." Camperdown is cited for its "fine presentation of local theatre, with excellent costume set and acting by the cast."

The school delights in the fact that past student Sylvia (Henry) Ashley is named by the Kingston Chapter of the Jamaica Secretaries Association as "Secretary of the Year for 1978."

A statue of Donald Quarrie is unveiled at the entrance to the National Stadium. Quarrie is recognized as the "speed king of the 1970s."

Chess: The Camperdown Chess Club is inaugurated and maintains a busy schedule during the year.

Cricket: Camperdown wins the 30-over Tappin Cup Knock-out competition, defeating Kingston Technical High School by 9 wickets. It is a first for the school in cricket. Camperdown is also a semi-finalist in the Sunlight Cup competition. The squad comprises Earl Melbourne (Captain), Dennis Gordon, Dave Harris, Patrick Dawes, Carlton Williams, Adrian Faulkner, Astley Crawford, Donald Davidson, Percival Tomlinson, Thomas McLean, Wayne Stoddart, Seiveright Meggoe, Michael Deans, Donald Morrison, and Errol Taylor. Earl Melbourne is selected as a member of the West Indies Youth Team to tour England.

Camperdown is also in the final of the Colts Competition and loses to Jamaica College.

Athletics: Girls' Champs – Audrey Llewellyn-Hunter (previously Audrey Llewellyn) wins the Class 1 High Jump, is 2nd in the Long Jump, 3rd in the 100m hurdles, and is champion girl in Class 1 with 15 points. Camperdown finishes in 11th place.

Boys' Champs: Camperdown (6th place) wins the Class 3 4x100m relay. Fenton Hugg wins the Class 3 400m in a new record of 51.7secs; he is 2nd in the 200m.

At the Carifta Games in the Bahamas, former Camperdown sprinter, Emmett DeCambre, wins the U-17 Boys 200m in 21.16 seconds, a record that would stand for 25 years until broken in 2002 by Usain Bolt.

Football: Patrick "Jackie" Walters is successful in his first coaching job at the schoolboy level and Camperdown registers its first hold on the coveted Manning Cup, defeating Tivoli Gardens High School, 1 – 0, in the final, with a goal by Thomas McLean. The school goes on to share the Olivier Shield with Clarendon College. The 19 members of the squad are: Carlton Williams (Captain), Anthony Lewis, Gladstone Heron, Ripton White, Kevin Purrier, Eric Maynard, Lloyd Crawford, Thomas McLean (Vice Captain), Donald Morrison, Barrington Edwards, Errol Blake, Donovan Lambert, Patrick Dawes, Wayne Williams, Kenneth Henry, Peter Trail, Delroy Lewis, Wayne James, and Samuel Duncan.

Thomas McLean is seen as "the driving force behind the team." The inventive Errol Blake, called "The Scarlett Pimpernel" by adoring fans, is described as the best dribbler in the Manning Cup competition.

Five Camperdown players are named to the All-Manning squad: Carlton Williams, Anthony Lewis, Thomas McLean, Barrington Edwards, and Errol Blake,

1979: The social situation in the country continues to deteriorate, and student attendance is negatively impacted as parents are afraid to send their children to school in a climate of crime and violence. During the year, four Camperdown students lose parents to gun violence and some students fear attending school due to threats against their lives.

In this climate of fear and intimidation, students are held-up on campus and robbed of their belongings. This is by no means a problem only at Camperdown; it is a country-wide problem, though more pronounced in the urban areas. Despite this, school morale on the whole remains high and more students are opting to do Advanced Level work.

There are further problems with the shift system as schools are experiencing additional difficulties in finding suitable teachers for certain subjects. In some areas, teachers are forced to do double shifts, in some cases teaching full-time on one shift and part-time on the other.

Over the period 1979-80, the syllabus is further modernized in Home Economics and now includes areas as Food and Nutrition, Textiles and Clothing, Construction, Home Management, Family Life Education, and Child Care.

In the Secondary Schools Drama Festival, Camperdown's entry, "The Position," receives an award for "special costume." The play is written by past student, Richard Blackford (Head Boy, 1975-76).

Athletics: Camperdown ends Boys' Champs in 6th place; the girls place 11th as star athlete, Audrey Llewellyn-Hunter, is champion girl, winning the Class 1 100m Hurdles, the High Jump, and the Long Jump. She also placed 2nd in the Shot Put. In the Class 1 Hurdles, Sharon Moffat runs a record 14.3s in the heats, but loses in the final to teammate Llewellyn-Hunter in a slower time.

At the Carifta Games in Jamaica, Fenton Hugg wins gold medals in the U-17 Boys 400m and 800m. Sharon Moffat wins the gold medal in the U-20 Women 100m Hurdles, while Audrey Llewellyn-Hunter wins the gold medal in the U-20 Women Long Jump.

Football: Camperdown and Clarendon College (joint holders of the Olivier Shield) participate in a special match at the National Stadium to raise funds in aid of the "International Year of the Child."

Camperdown wins the Manning Cup for the second year in succession, beating Ardenne 3 – 0 in the final on goals by Delroy Lewis, Errol Blake, and Eric Maynard. Blake and Maynard are the outstanding players. The game is watched by 25,000 spectators. They win the Olivier Shield for the second consecutive year, defeating Dinthill Technical High School by a cumulative score of 3 – 0 in the two-match playoff. In the first match played in Ewarton, they win 2-0 on goals by Errol Blake and Delroy Lewis. In the return match at the National Stadium, they win 1-0 on Blake's goal.

The team is acknowledged in *The Daily Gleaner* (December 7, 1979): "Camperdown proved themselves the best, the fittest, and the most sporting team in the competition."

Despite these successes, Camperdown again fails to win the Walker Cup, losing to Calabar High School in the semi-finals.

Members of the 1979 squad are: Carlton Williams (Captain), Kenneth Henry (Vice-Captain), Eric Maynard, Michael Brown, Delroy Lewis, Lloyd Crawford, Peter Hibbert, Everton Grant, Ronald Headlam, Errol Myrie, Richard Gordon, Peter Trail, Patrick Dawes, Dean Davidson, Gladstone Heron, Peter Cargill, Mark Salmon, Donovan Corcho, Errol Blake, and Richard Green.

Six members of the team – Williams, Henry, Corcho, Blake, Maynard, and Crawford are chosen for the All-Manning and All-Schools teams. Williams, called "Spiderman" because of his acrobatic brilliance in goal, wins acclaim as "Camperdown's brilliant goalkeeper…and the master of excellent judgment between the sticks." He is chosen as captain of both teams.

Cricket: As defending champion, Camperdown is in the semi-final of the Tappin Knockout Cup competition, but loses to Calabar at Kensington Park. Top players are pace bowler Percival Tomlinson, now a Benson and Hedges Youth player, Patrick Dawes, Donald Morrison, spinner Harris Hamilton, and batsmen Carlton Williams and Dave Harris. Hamilton also represents the Kingston Cricket Club during the season. The season is marked by the history-making performance of Courtney Walsh. Playing for Excelsior High School in the Sunlight Cup match against Camperdown, Walsh takes all 10 Camperdown wickets in the innings (10 for 43), leading Excelsior to a

MAJOR BUILDING YEARS: 1960s – 1970s

3-wicket victory, and giving him his first claim to fame.

Tomlinson is invited to trial for the All-Sunlight team; he goes on to represent Jamaica at the senior level in the 1980/1981 season.

Three years later, Walsh is a Jamaica representative, and by 1984 he is playing for the West Indes.

Chess: The Chess Club maintains a busy schedule during the year and is 5th in the zone. Leading players are the team's captain, Aneft Budhai (Head Boy—1979-80), Bryan Brown, Lloyd Crawford, Dennis Howard, Bryan Peart, and Michael Walker.

Past student, Franklyn Williams, is elected Councillor for Independence City in the St. Catherine Parish Council.

The first two decades of the "new" (grant-aided) Camperdown, though laden with obstacles and challenges, were used in laying the foundation to lift the school up the ladder of prominence among the country's leading high schools. The promise of future advances reflected the wildly-held view that Camperdown was on the move. In this atmosphere of heightened euphoria there was no stopping the progress. It all depended on the students and faculty to continue the sustained strides into a glorious future.

The students attending Camperdown during these two foundational decades would come to be seen as "the exceptional generation."

4

Solum Optima: *To Seek the Best*

The momentum built and successes of the preceding two decades incited further challenges and opportunities. Indeed, the Camperdown community dared to continue on its path-breaking drive to excellence. Added effort was concentrated on the academic side; it was also a foregone conclusion that an equally great effort would be placed on extra-curricular activities. It became clear that to stay in the consciousness of the Jamaican society, the school would have to remain highly engaged in sporting activities, with football and athletics at the forefront. Even though the school by the decade of the 1980s was highly recognized in athletics, particularly in the sprinting events, where the smaller schools are concerned, winning Champs was clearly not a viable option. In the minds of many, winning Champs has been manipulated away from the smaller schools. Outside of track and field, from as early as the mid-seventies, Camperdown had shown that it could be competitive, and by the late 1970s had risen to the highest level in schoolboy football, winning both the Manning Cup and the Olivier Shield, the emblems of schoolboy supremacy. By 1979, Camperdown was the defending high school football champion.

1980: The society continues to be plagued by tragic and sustained violence affecting all strata, including the schools. National elections are in the air, and in the turbulent atmosphere of the times, hundreds are killed in the run-up to the elections.

Enrollment is now 1,450 students—842 girls and 608 boys.

Sharon Grant, a 6th Former, is excited to take first place in the essay competition organized by the United Nations Food and Agriculture Organization (FAO). In the GCE Ordinary Level examination, encouraging passes come in Additional Mathematics and Chemistry. At the Advanced Level, good passes are obtained in Mathematics, English and History; at CXC Level, strong passes are shown in Mathematics, History, Geography, Principles of Business, Accounts and Typewriting.

Drama: The school's play is well received in the annual Secondary Schools Drama Festival and medals are won in group and individual singing.

A new house is organized and Quarrie House (Colour – Orange) is named in honour of Olympic Gold, Silver, and Bronze medalist, Donald Quarrie.

Camperdown benefits from sponsorship from the Guinness Company to produce the school's calendar for the year, featuring the championship football teams of 1978 and 1979.

Football: Camperdown is in the final of the Manning Cup for the third consecutive year, and loses in extra time to Excelsior High School by a score of 1-0.

Athletics: At Boys' Champs, Camperdown finishes 3rd out of 41 competing schools. Leroy Reid wins the Class 1 200 metre in 21.7 seconds. Other excellent performances come from top athletes Fenton Hugg (1st in Class 2 800m, 2nd in 400m), Raymond Ramsey (3rd in Class 1 400m), and Patrick Cunningham, winner of the Class 2 200m and 400m. Camperdown is 2nd in the Class 1 Boys 4x100m relay in 41.9s, wins the Class 2 Boys 4x100m relay in 42.7s, and 2nd in the Class 3 Boys 4x100m in 45.6 seconds. In Class 3, Lloyd Mingoes wins the 100m and is 2nd in the 200m.

After an 11th place finish in 1979 Champs, the girls end at 23rd in 1980 (tied with York Castle and St. Elizabeth Technical High schools).

The school participates in two other top-class meets during the season – the Gibson Relays (held at the National Stadium) and the Penn Relays in Philadelphia. On both occasions the team delivers excellent performances, in keeping with the school's motto that "Only the Best is Good Enough."

At the Penn Relays, Camperdown wins the only gold medal obtained by a Jamaican high school as the team of Howard Lawrence, Wayne Morrison,

Oswald Cole, and Leroy Reid wins the Boys 4x100m relay in a new record time of 41.3 seconds, on course to becoming the most dominant Jamaican high school team at the Relays during the decade of the 1980s. Audrey Llewellyn-Hunter takes bronze medals in the girls' High Jump and Long Jump.

In the Relay of Champions meet at the National Stadium, Camperdown wins the Class 1 Boys 4x100m relay in 41.4 seconds; in the Boys Class 3 4x100m relay they win in a time of 45.1 seconds.

At the Carifta Games in Bermuda, Reid wins the gold medal in the U-20 Men's 200m and the bronze medal in the 100m.

During the month of September, the service celebrating the 50th Anniversary of the school is held at the St. Andrew Scots Kirk Church. The main address is given by the Moderator of the United Church, Reverend Dr. H.D. Swaby.

1981: The school continues to grow and there are now 74 full-time members of staff. Staffing continues to be problematic as teachers leave for better-paying jobs elsewhere in Jamaica or leave simply to migrate.

Senior teachers, Mrs. Diane Mayne and Mrs. Myrtle Kellier, act as Vice-Principals as Mrs. Winifred Smith and Mr. Stanley Williams are both on leave. Their period of acting is recognized for being outstanding in terms of "cooperation, dedication and efficiency."

Champs: Girls—Camperdown places 25th.

Boys—Much is expected and Camperdown places 3rd at Boys' Champs, which ends prematurely due to an incident involving Calabar High School and Kingston College. Leroy Reid is the winner of the Class 1 100m and 200m. He runs 10.3 seconds in the 100m to break the old record. Camperdown also wins the Class 1 4x100m relay in 41.2 seconds.

At the Gibson Relays at the National Stadium, Camperdown wins the Boys 4x100m relay in 41.1 seconds.

At the Penn Relays, the Camperdown team of Howard Lawrence, Wayne Morrison, Oswald Cole, and Leroy Reid breaks the record they set one year ago in winning the 4x100m relay in a new record time by running 40.9 seconds. This is how that historic win was described:

From the start the result was never in any doubt as Lawrence's rocket start coupled with an impeccable baton change with Morrison put Camperdown in an unbeatable position. However, Cole and Reid were not contented with the established lead, and Cole opened the full throttle to hand over to Reid. With an anchorman of the calibre of Reid there was no hope of the other teams improving their position against Camperdown. With no opposition Reid unleashed a merciless assault on what was left of the old record of 41.34 which was set by the same team the year before.

At the Carifta Games in the Bahamas, Reid wins gold in the U-20 Men 100m, becoming only the third Jamaican to win this event in the ten years of the competition. He also takes the silver medal in the 200m. In the U-17 Boys category, Raymond Stewart wins gold medals in the 100m and 200m.

Coach Glen Mills is highlighted as he guides his small team to sit atop the high schools' sprinting pantheon. The school comes to dominate the sprinting events at Champs and the Penn Relays. With sprinters as Donald Quarrie, Anthony Attride, Michael Murray, Godfrey Murray, Rodney Fitz-Gordon, Eric Barrett, Edward Quarrie, Peter Hibbert, Leroy Reid, and Raymond Stewart, Camperdown cements its place as the "Sprint Factory."

Based on its new record and dominance at the Penn Relays, Principal Jeff Brown, Coach Glen Mills, and the team members are invited to meet with the Minister of Sports, Honourable Errol Anderson. Past student, Fidelia (Johnson) Thaws, was responsible for organizing the effort through voluntary contributions to fund the team's journey to the Penn Relays in 1980 and 1981.

Lower 6th Form student Ray Palmer's invention – a gadget that he named "HYDRO GYRO" – an instrument to assist in the navigation of aircraft, is submitted to the United States Association of Inventors, who concludes that it is of "marketable value."

1982: This is the year that the pundits expect Camperdown to win Champs, as both Kingston College and Calabar High School are banned from the competition for the year. But disappointment again rears its ugly head. Top sprinter Leroy Reid comes up with an injury and his absence will cause the school to lose many valuable points in the 100m and 200m sprints and in the 4x100m and 4x400m relays. Camperdown again finishes in 2nd position.

THE STORY OF CAMPERDOWN HIGH SCHOOL

In this his first year in Class 1, Raymond Stewart places 2nd in the 100m and 3rd in the 200m. Fenton Hugg wins the Class 1 400m; Patrick Cunningham takes 3rd place, while Lloyd Mingoes wins the Class 2 200m and places 2nd in the 100m. Camperdown also wins the Class 2 4x100m relay.

At the Carifta Games in Jamaica, Shane Howell wins gold in the U-17 Boys 100m. In the U-17 Girls, Laurel Johnson wins gold in the 100m and 200m.

The year brings with it a number of changes. Mr. Jeff Brown, Principal since taking over from Mrs. Grant in 1968, retires and passes leadership of the school to Mrs. Winifred Smith, first in an acting capacity when Jeff Brown was out on sick leave in mid-1982, until confirmation as Principal in 1983.

Winifred Josephine Smith comes to the task as the first Camperdown past student to assume leadership of the school. Smith (nee Winifred Crooks) attended Camperdown for two years – 1949 to 1950. After passing the Senior Cambridge School Certificate examination, she attended Excelsior High School to sit the Higher School Certificate examination. Smith was born in Santiago, Cuba, to Jamaican parents who had migrated there, and came to Jamaica with her parents at the age of eight.

She attended St. Michael Primary School before Camperdown and then went on to Excelsior. The route from St. Michael to Camperdown was established and facilitated by the closeness of teachers in both institutions, but particularly through the effort of Mrs. Nora Malcolm, whose sister also taught at St. Michael. The route from Camperdown to Excelsior was possible because of the close family ties between Mrs. Grant and Mr. Powell, both from strong Seventh-day Adventist families.

After gaining the Higher School Certificate, Smith taught for three years (1952-1955) at Merl Grove High School. She then studied for the B.A. degree and the Diploma in Education at the University of the West Indies. She later received the M.A. degree in Educational Administration from the same university.

According to Smith, teaching at Camperdown was one of the highlights of her professional life. It was as a student at Camperdown that she came under the influence of Mrs. Grant, seeing first-hand the lessons of care and discipline, which she carried with her throughout her career. Smith (Miss Crooks or "Crooksie" to her earlier students) is remembered as the "consummate teacher of English and English Literature" by her former students.

An outstanding educator, she was to give 33 years of service to the school (1959 to 1992). She also served as Treasurer of ISSA.

As Principal, Smith continued to build on the foundation laid by Ivy Grant and Jeff Brown in the expansion of the school. In the process, Camperdown becomes one of the most recognized high schools in Jamaica, not merely in academics, but also in the physical, social and spiritual spheres. The curriculum is expanded to engage students in typing, accounting, business and other technical subjects. Buildings are renovated and refurbished to cater to the growing student body. In 1985, premises on Portland Road are purchased to widen the boundaries of the school. New classrooms are put in place to increase the available Sixth Form spaces and to provide accommodation for the "Operation English" project to be housed at Camperdown.

During the decade, the student population continues to expand, moving close to the 2,000 mark. This calls for the expansion of the academic and administrative staff and witnesses an increasing number of past students holding administrative and academic positions at their alma mater.

By 1984, the academic staff included 66 full-time and 29 part-time members. Numbered among the teaching and administrative staff, there are 11 past students. To manage the situation, the school's two shifts are under the leadership of Mrs. Myrtle Kellier and Mr. Ralph Williams. The 15 academic departments include Mathematics, Business Education, English, Spanish and French, History, Home Economics, Religious Education, Physical Education, Geography, Science, Technical Studies, Music, Drama, Art and Craft, and Guidance and Counseling, with improved results in many subject areas. Students also participated in a growing number of extra-curricular activities – Inter-Schools Christian Fellowship, Science Club, Key Club, Girls' Guide, Cadet Corps, Spanish Club, Schools Challenge Quiz,

Science Exhibitions, and National Art and Craft among the most prominent. A Junior Achievement Club and a Red Cross Club are formed. A Steel Band is also organized.

In the Erwin Burgine Literary Competition of 1983, student Valentine Bailey wins 2nd place with the short story, "Exploitation." Another student, Gary Blinth (Head Boy – 1985-86), is also a 2nd place winner of the same competition in 1985. During the period, a Development Committee under the leadership of Mr. William McLeod is launched. A fundraising drive is also undertaken, including a "Buy a Block Drive," a newspaper and bottle collection drive, and ending with a grand fair. Not to be left out, the Parent/Teachers Association organizes a fundraising drive with the Annual Supper and Tag Drive. The school also receives a commitment from a private-sector company, VGC Holdings, to furnish a classroom with desks and chairs.

The class of 1983, comprising 308 Fifth Form graduates and 40 "6A" graduates, stands out as a number of those graduating go on to meaningful careers or make important contributions to the country's sports teams. Numbered among those graduates are Rainford Wint (Head Boy – 1984-85), Allan Cunningham, Peter Ruddock, Trevor Chambers, Valentine Bailey, Teddence Bailey, Christopher Bender, Barrington Gaynor, Shane Howell, and Ricardo Hyde. Among them, also, are future Olympians, Raymond Stewart and Andrew Smith.

At the Penn Relays in 1983, Camperdown wins the Boys 4x100m relay (Fitzroy Stephenson, Raymond Stewart, Hugh Fyffe, and Shane Howell), is 2nd in the 4x400m, and is also 2nd in the 4x800m, highlighted by Franklyn Salkey's anchor leg of 1:53.2 seconds.

By 1985, the shift system is phased out and replaced with an experimental "overlap" or "staggered" system, whereby students would enter school at two different times in the morning – 7:30am and 10:30am – with the school day ending at 3:00pm rather than at 5:00pm, to allow for fuller participation by all students in extra-curricular activities.

By 1986, Camperdown reverts to a single system with additional forms in Grades 7-9 and Grades 10-11, which were grouped into Arts, Science,

Technical, and Business options. French and Computer Science are introduced in the curriculum between 1986 and 1987.

In sports, the decade of the eighties proves a glorious one for the school as Camperdown takes the "Triple Crown" in 1982—Manning Cup, Olivier Shield and Walker Cup—for the first time in its history. This is seen as the greatest single sporting moment in the school's history.

In the Manning Cup final they beat Kingston College 2 – 0, and in the Walker Cup defeated Wolmer's by a score of 3 – 0. Richard Green is credited with scoring one of the best goals of the schoolboy season in the victory over Wolmer's. The squad of 17 included: Peter Cargill (Captain), Mark Salmon, Michael Clarke, George Malcolm, Richard Green, Andrew Hines, Barrington Gaynor, Nyron Prawl, Prince Topey, Ricardo Hyde, Christopher Bender, Steve Nelson, Claude Palmer, Dale Palmer, Carl Herbert, Winston Campbell, and Carl Richards.

In the two-leg Olivier Shield final, Camperdown defeated Cornwall College by an aggregate score of 2-1. Only two goals are scored against Camperdown in the entire 1982 season, a powerful testament to the all-consuming power and brilliance of the football team; it ranks as one of the greatest achievements in the history of schoolboy football in Jamaica.

Seven Camperdown players are named to the 1982 All-Manning team – Peter Cargill, Barrington Gaynor, Andrew Hines, Richard Green, Dale Palmer, Mark Salmon, and Nyron Prawl.

Peter Cargill, the leading goal-scorer in the Manning Cup, and Michael Clarke are suspended at the end of the season for disciplinary reasons. Weakened by the absence of these two players, plus still recovering from the euphoria of winning the "triple," Camperdown loses 2-1 in extra time to Vere Technical High School in the inaugural Nutrament Shield at the National Stadium. The Nutrament Shield is contested by the winners of the Corporate Area Walker Cup and the rural area Ben Francis Knockout Cup.

Peter Cargill and Richard Green are selected to represent the Jamaica juvenile team in the Caribbean Football Union tournament.

The 1982 team was honoured and inducted into the school's "Hall of Fame" in 2013 at a function hosted by the Camperdown Past Students Association (St. Andrew Chapter – CASTAC) at the Pegasus Hotel in Kingston. The team's outstanding coach, Mr. Jackie Walters, who also led Camperdown to Manning Cup and Olivier Shield championships in 1978 and 1979, was honoured with the Ivy Grant Award for his outstanding contribution to the school and many football titles won.

Four Camperdown players are selected to the 1983 All-Manning team – George Malcolm, Dominique Spalding, Ricardo Hyde, and Barrington Gaynor.

In 1985, Camperdown is in the Walker Cup final but loses 3-0 to Kingston College.

Throughout the rest of the 1980s, the school continues to excel in different areas, particularly in football. Top players include Adonis Maxwell, Troy Pinnock, Carlton Simmonds, Fitzroy Jackson, and Dane Walker, all members of the 1988 Manning Cup team. The 1988 team is seen by many (Coach Walters included) as the best Camperdown team ever, but one that was not successful in winning any of the major trophies that year. As consolation, Camperdown wins the less-coveted Walker Cup in 1988, defeating Charlie Smith High School 2-0, on goals by Maxwell and Jackson.

Camperdown also contests for the Nutrament Shield against Herbert Morrison Comprehensive High School.

Camperdown's invitees to the 1988 All-Manning team are Adonis Maxwell, Fitzroy Jackson, Dane Walker, and Carlton Simmonds. Invitees to the 1989 All-Manning team are Garfield Robinson, Fitzroy Jackson, and Dane Walker.

In athletics, the boys' team continued its strong tradition at Champs, ending at 2nd in 1983 and 3rd in 1984 and 1985, 6th in 1986, 6th in 1987, 5th in 1989, 8th in 1990 (tied with Munro College).

At Champs, Raymond Stewart in 1983 wins the 100/200m sprint double in Class 1; Garfield Campbell does likewise in Class 2.

At the 1983 Carifta Games in Martinique, Stewart wins the gold medal in the U-20 Men 200m; he also takes the silver medal in the 100m. In the U-17 Girls 100m, Laurel Johnson takes the silver medal.

In 1984, Stewart repeats his fantastic sprint double at Champs, as well as winning the gold medal in the U-20 Men 100m at the Carifta Games in the Bahamas. Stewart would go on to hold the Jamaica Junior 100m record of 10.0 seconds for 23 years.

SOLUM OPTIMA: TO SEEK THE BEST

A most fitting tribute to the school was cemented when Raymond Stewart, only a few months after his Champs conquests, and Donald Quarrie, both Camperdown icons, carried the Jamaica team to win the silver medal in the 4x100m relay at the Olympic Games in Los Angeles in 1984. Stewart at 19 years old, was the youngest runner in the final of the 100m, finishing 6th in the 8-man final. Donald Quarrie was participating in his 5th Olympics, a rare achievement for a world-class sprinter. Stewart, the first Jamaican to break the 10.0s barrier in the 100m, would also make the Olympic finals in 1988 (7th place) and 1992 (7th place), the first man to appear in three consecutive Olympic 100m finals. As a reminder of his greatness as a sprinter, Stewart also made four consecutive 100m finals in the World Athletics Championships.

In 1985, the Boys' Softball team wins three trophies, including "most disciplined" and "best dressed" team.

At the Penn Relays that year (1985), Camperdown's team of Michael Warren, Fitzroy Stephenson, Carey Johnson, and Alexander Strachan wins the Boys' 4x400m relay in a new record time of 3:11.4 seconds, accomplishing a feat that had eluded any team from Jamaica for over eight years. Camperdown is second in the 4x100m relay, but is disqualified for passing the baton outside the zone.

At the Carifta Games (1985) in Barbados, Carey Johnson wins the U-17 Boys 400m.

In 1986, the Camperdown boys win all three sprint events in Class 1 – Garfield Campbell (100m and 200m) and Carey Johnson (400m).

The girls' team, on the other hand, places 5th at Champs in 1986, and wins the Mortimer Geddes Achievement Trophy for most improved school.

At the Carifta Games in Guadeloupe (1986), Laurel Johnson (now attending St. Jago High School) takes bronze medals in the U-20 Women 100m and 200m.

In Girls' Champs (1987), the team placed 4th overall and retained the trophy as the Corporate area champions. Revolie Campbell was Class 3 champion at Girls' Champs, winning the 200m and 400m. She was brilliant at the Mutual Life Games. Campbell was the outstanding female athlete at the 1987 Miami International Games in Florida. Along with teammates Andria Lloyd, Marie Taylor and Ann Marie Bonthrone, they capture eight medals, including four golds. For her brilliant display at the Mutual Games in Jamaica, she was awarded a $2,000 scholarship to use toward her high school education. In 1988 she was the U-16 champion girl for the second year in succession.

At the Carifta Games in Trinidad that same year (1987), Campbell wins gold medals in the U-17 Girls 200m and 400m, while her school-mate, Andria Lloyd, takes the silver in the U-17 Girls 100m and 200m. At the 1988 Carifta Games in Jamaica, Campbell again takes the U-17 Girls 200m and 400m.

The girls continued their impressive show at various athletic meets. In Champs 1989, they ended in 4th place. Lloyd takes the sprint double (100m and 200m) in Class 1, as Camperdown wins the Douglas Saint Memorial Trophy as the top girls' school from the Corporate area. The duo of Andria Lloyd and Revolie Campbell was on a formidable path.

Campbell continues the onslaught at Champs in 1990, winning both 100m and 200m in Class 1, with teammate Vinette Phillips placing 2nd in both races. Campbell runs 23.2secs in the 200m to break the old record held by Merlene Ottey. Maxine Dawkins in Class 3 also takes the sprint double, establishing a new record of 24.3s in the 200m.

Camperdown finishes in 4th place at Champs in 1990, winning the Milo Trophy as the top Corporate Area team. Camperdown again places 4th in 1991.

Campbell's dominance is heralded as she continues to give outstanding performances. At the Comet Relays in Montego Bay, Camperdown is awarded the Sydney "Foggy" Burrowes Trophy as the most outstanding female team, and Campbell is voted the most outstanding female athlete of the meet. Here is a telling reminder of Campbell's brilliance at that year's (1990) Comet Relays (***The Daily Gleaner***, February 12, 1990):

> Campbell got her award for two great relay legs. In the sprint relay she handed over [the] baton first on the back stretch after receiving it in second to last position. However, her greatest run came in the 4x200m Open [relay] as she took her team from a hopeless position to a dramatic victory. In what must rank as one of her best ever runs, Campbell, running the anchor leg, got the baton some twenty metres behind Vere's Merlene Fraser and St. Jago's Marjorie Bailey. She brought the large crowd to their feet as she demonstrated her true fighting ability by making up tremendous ground to pass her two opponents some 25 metres from home.

SOLUM OPTIMA: TO SEEK THE BEST

At the 1990 running of the Miami Classics, twin sisters Maxine and Marlene Dawkins, turn in superlative performances to again underline the tremendous sprinting capacity the school is known for.

But Revolie Campbell's most outstanding performances are at the Penn Relays. Under coach Raymond "KC" Graham, who coached the Camperdown girls' team from 1985 to 1992, the girls were dominant in the sprints and in the relays. The Camperdown girls first appeared at the Penn Relays in 1988, promptly placing 3rd in the 4x100m relay. With Campbell leading the charge, Camperdown wins the 4x100m relay at the Penn Relays in 1989 and 1990. After placing second to Vere Technical High School in 1991, Camperdown is again victorious in 1992, winning the 4x100m relay in 45.37 seconds.

At the 1989 renewal of the Gibson Relays, the girls team runs 46.2s to win the 4x100m relay. Following that, they run 45.5s at the National Relay carnival, breaking the U-19 record held by Vere. Surprisingly, the title was taken from them after a protest by Vere, which objected that the Camperdown team had used 16-year old Revolie Campbell, and should thus be disqualified as she (Campbell) was too young to participate in that particular event. Surprisingly, the protest was upheld!

Undeterred, after this it was off to the Penn Relays.

The Camperdown girls created history at the Penn Relays in 1989 when the team of Marie Taylor, Helena Rochester, Revolie Campbell and Andria Lloyd blazed the track at Franklin Field to win the Championship 4x100m relay in a new record time of 45.13 seconds, beating the old record of 45.57 seconds set by Vere in 1987.

At the Carifta Games that year in Barbados (1989), Campbell wins the U-20 Women 200m, while Andria Lloyd takes the bronze medal. Lloyd also wins the silver medal in the U-20 Women 100m, while Campbell wins the bronze medal.

At the Carifta Games in Jamaica in 1990, Campbell wins the gold medal in the U-20 Women 100m and 200m, while Maxine Dawkins wins the silver medal in the U-17 Girls 200m.

At the Penn Relays (1990), Camperdown successfully defends its title in the Girls' 4x100m relay (Marie Taylor, Revolie Campbell, Vinette Phillips, Maxine Dawkins). Camperdown's Marlene Cole also takes 2nd place in the Long Jump.

The cricket team, though producing some good players, withdraws from the Sunlight Cup competition in 1988; the school did not enter a team in 1989.

Other notable achievements continued in the arts as well as in sports. Not to be overlooked, the Drama Group wins a gold medal at the National Drama Festival, while the Dance Team under the leadership of Miss June Watson continued to give impressive performances.

Two teachers of Mathematics, Mrs. Cynthia Cooke and Mrs. Annette Henry, collaborate on a text book, "Mathematics: Multiple Choice/Objective Questions," published by McMillan Caribbean Company, for use by students in preparing for the CXC Examinations.

In 1986, Mr. William L. McLeod was named as Chairman of the Board of Governors.

In 1986, the Camperdown Association of Social Intervention (CASI) was founded to underline students' interest in social upliftment, helping to prepare them for the world of work, and covering such areas as public speaking, deportment, planning and executing social functions and other civic engagements. The association also adopted the Marigold Children's Home and made visits to the home, putting into practice the ideals of good and caring citizenship. The school also joined the American Field Service (AFS) High School Exchange Programme, an initiative geared to increase youth understanding. In 1988, three students, all members of CASI, were selected as part of a group of 30 Jamaican students to spend a year abroad, living with local host families and attending local high schools as a way of "living the culture" and learning about other cultures and countries. The three students – George Scott in Colombia, Jacqueline Wilson in Sweden, and Nadine Samuels in Canada – benefited tremendously from their participation. The Camperdown CASI programme operated under the leadership of teacher, Miss Sonia Bennett.

Camperdown students also entered the annual "Teens Star Search Talent Contest," opened to high school students and youth club members. Camperdown students excelled in these competitions. They were exposed to the dynamics of the competition, competing in Pop, Rock, Gospel, Reggae,

SOLUM OPTIMA: TO SEEK THE BEST

Jazz, Country and Western categories. In the 1989 competition, Lloyd Edwards wins the award as "Best Dressed Performer." Althea Hewitt competed in solo in the "pop" song category, winning the 3rd prize and a $1,000 award, which was shared with the school. It was in this competition that famed gospel singer, Sandra Llewellyn, was discovered in 1988, competing in the gospel song category. Llewellyn was praised as possessing a "very strong and impressive voice [vibrant, soul-searching and revealing] which should take her places."

Sandra Llewellyn, who led many morning worship sessions at school, went on to become the lead singer of the national and international gospel group, The Grace Thrillers. She became an ordained Evangelist and gained worldwide recognition and appearances with some of the most famous gospel acts. Althea Hewitt went on to record a number of songs that did well on the popular charts.

Overall, there was noticeable improvement in exam results, with best grades coming in Chemistry, History, and General Paper at Advanced Level, and Additional Mathematics, Religious Education and Computer Science at Ordinary Level.

In 1986, the boys' track team created history at the Penn Relays, when the team of Derrick Thomas, Carey Johnson, Ralston Wright and Garfield Campbell did 40.43 seconds to break the record in the 4x100m relay. In the Mutual Life Games in Jamaica they win the 4x100m relay in a similar time. At the Carifta Games in Guadeloupe, Garfield Campbell wins the bronze medal in the U-20 Men 100m.

In the Secondary Schools Drama Festival in 1987, Camperdown's entry, "Cousin Adriana Coming," directed by Winston Bell, is well received and acknowledged as being "outstanding." It is described as "a domestic comedy," and "the result was convincing realism." The school's success continues in the World Health Day programme, winning the 16-19 age group Poster Competition. In the Junior Achievement Programme at the Wyndham Hotel, Janice Elliott is chosen to deliver the valedictory address, and in the ICWI National Schools Safety Week Exhibition, Camperdown students receive special prizes for "most outstanding posters."

In Champs (1987), the Girls' team finishes in 4th place and the Boys' team finishes in 6th place. At the Carifta Games that year in Trinidad, Carey Johnson wins the silver medal in the U-20 Men 200m. Both Boys' and

Girls' teams participated in other meets in Jamaica and overseas – in Florida (Orlando and Miami), the Penn Relays in Philadelphia, and in the Junior Games in Sudbury, Canada.

In 1988, a number of fundraising activities are organized and, to cope with increased costs, fees are increased to cover the expanding book rental scheme and to provide a small stipend to teachers as an added incentive.

In 1989, 6th Form student, Lorraine Hunter, is awarded a 2-year scholarship to read for the Associate Degree in Hotel Management at the University of Maine in the United States.

Several areas of the school, mostly roofs and fences, had to be repaired in 1989 due to the damage caused by Hurricane Gilbert. As a result, the Camperdown High School Trust Fund was launched at the Lincoln United Church to attract funds for repair and development work at the school. Three new classrooms were dedicated at a function at which the British High Commissioner was the Guest Speaker.

In 1990, Prime Minister Michael Manley was the Guest Speaker at the school's Graduation and Prize-Giving Ceremony at the Jamaica Conference Centre. There were 128 graduates.

During the year 1991, the Honourable Carlyle Dunkley, Minister of Education, and other officials from the Ministry of Education, visited the school for the ground-breaking ceremony for the new English Language Resource Centre, which would provide accommodation for administrative and technological facilities to support "Operation English." The Centre, a gift of the Rotary Club of Kingston and a hallmark project of the school's chairman, received a collection of books donated by the United States Information Service and the Van Leer company, coinciding with the new Religious Education syllabus of the CXC. The Centre's "Operation English" is aimed at improving competency in written and oral English among Camperdown students. The launch of the Centre was addressed by Governor General, Sir Florizel Glasspole, a long-time supporter of the school.

The Service marking the 60th Anniversary of the school (1930-1990), held at St. Andrew Scots Kirk Church, was addressed by Reverend Douglas Miller. The Guest Speaker for the occasion was the Minister of Education.

SOLUM OPTIMA: TO SEEK THE BEST

The decades of the 1980's and 1990's witnessed the continuing decline in the social and economic situation in Jamaica. An increasing number of students had to fend for themselves as their parents migrated to other countries to cope with the decline. Many students needed assistance with lunch money and other incidentals. Added to this was the declining recruitment and retention of qualified teachers, particularly in subjects such as Mathematics, Physics, English and Geography.

In 1989, Camperdown wins the Corporate Area Games Mistresses Association Junior Netball title by defeating Ardenne, 16 – 14, in the final. The victorious team members were: Tashi Williams (Captain), Kerry Ann Bailey, Peta Gaye McKenzie, Keisha Robinson, Debbie Ann Hall, and Hilda Gordon.

During the 1990s, the school continued on a gradually upward trajectory. The academic programme remained relevant with encouraging results, and extra-curricular activities were a constant part of the students' workload. For example, Diana Campbell was awarded a scholarship in 1990 by the Cooperative Association of States for Scholarships (CASS) Programme for study in the United States. The curriculum was further enhanced with the introduction of Computer Studies at Ordinary Level. Sadly, the school mourned the loss of former Chairman, Mr. F.L. Sangster, a legendary figure in the growth and development of the school. The school also mourned the loss of Mr. Cyril Bell, a former Bursar, as well as a student, Floyd Barrett, who died after a period of illness. The school was represented at the funerals by members of the Board, staff and students.

In 1990, Camperdown was again in the final of the Manning Cup competition, losing to Charlie Smith in a tough match eventually decided on penalty kicks (4-3). Sadly, the match was marred by indiscipline. Camperdown's outstanding players were captain Peter Gordon, Darien Smith and Christopher Scott. Gordon was voted the Most Valuable Player in the Manning Cup competition for the year, winning the Jackie Bell Trophy for excellence, as well as a cash grant of five thousand dollars to help with his schooling. Gordon was also a member of the National Under-23 team. All three, plus Claude Hunt, were named to the All-Manning squad. Claude Hunt and Marklyn Anglin were also named to the Jamaica Under-17 football team, which participated in the CONCACAF tournament in Trinidad.

In 1991, Errol Byles, Gladston Morrison, and Leo Samuels represented

Jamaica at the Carifta Games in Trinidad. Samuels wins the silver medal in the U-17 Boys 800m. Byles wins the gold medal in the U-20 Men 100m Hurdles; he takes the silver medal in the 400m Hurdles. Morrison wins gold in the U-20 Men High Jump.

Byles and Maxine Dawkins are selected to the national team for the 1991 Pan American Junior Athletics Championships held in Kingston, with Dawkins winning a gold medal in the 4x100m relay.

By 1991, enrollment is at 1,338, with 661 boys and 677 girls.

***

The continuing social problems and years of disorder in the country escalate to the point where some students are without parental guidance and must fend for themselves. These societal problems now reach the transportation sector, affecting students who must travel great distances—from as far as the outer reaches of St. Thomas and St. Andrew. This results in additional problems for the school as tardiness and late arrivals mushroom. To remedy this, senior Mathematics teacher, Mrs. Cynthia Cooke, who also serves as the school's Dean of Discipline, imposes tough standards to counter this problem. Students who report late to school are now locked out and must report to the Principal's office. This and other anti-social behaviours are new and growing problems that schools now face.

By 1992, there are 1,350 students enrolled.

In the Jamaica Chamber of Commerce "Tourism Poster Competition," Steve Thomas captures the top prize in the 15-18 age group category. The aim of the competition is "to emphasize the importance of tourism to the country's economy."

At Champs (1992), Althea Green wins the Class 1 200m in a time of 24.9s. In Class 2, the Dawkins twins, Marlene and Maxine, are dominant. Marlene wins the 200m in 24.1s, followed by Maxine in 24.3s. Camperdown wins the Class 2 4x100m relay in 46.05s. In the Open 4x400m relay, Marlene collapses after running the first leg and had to be rushed to the hospital. She turned out to be fine, just exhausted.

At the Carifta Games in the Bahamas, Maxine Dawkins wins the bronze medal in the U-20 Women 200m.

At the Penn Relays, Camperdown is the winner of the girls' 4x100m relay (Althea Green, Maxine Dawkins, Bridgette Edwards, Marlene Dawkins).

In 1993, the school bids farewell to Principal, Mrs. Winifred Smith, who retires after 10 years in the position. In all she spent 33 years at Camperdown as teacher, Vice-Principal and Principal. She was hailed by the United Church "for distinguished service in many areas of church life" and as "an outstanding educator," who epitomizes the old Jamaican saying, "little but tallawah." The citation read at the farewell dinner in her honour noted that "her larger than life personality looms over the country's education fraternity where her life-long contribution has made a tremendous impact on the nation's development throughout her years of service at her alma mater. Under Smith's direction, Camperdown achieved an impressive list of accomplishments that remain the standard for other high schools with a longer history and much more resources."

Smith received the Order of Distinction (OD) from the Government of Jamaica "for service to Education" in 1992.

Mrs. Cynthia Cooke, another Camperdown past student, is named as Smith's replacement.

Cynthia Pamela (Warren) Cooke attended Camperdown from January 1961 to June 1966.

She attended Camperdown on scholarship from St. George's Girls School. After leaving Camperdown, she worked at the Government Medical Laboratory before attending the University of the West Indies. She returned to Camperdown in 1974 to teach Mathematics. By 1982, she was promoted to head the Mathematics Department as well as appointed as Dean of Discipline. Further studies were undertaken at Leeds University in the United Kingdom. In addition, between 1976 to 1984, she served as a part-time Lecturer at Excelsior Community College. She also served as an Examiner with the Caribbean Examination Council.

With an impressive background in Mathematics and Science, Cooke's interest in teaching and with helping children overcome learning disabilities, prompted her to author "New Comprehensive Math Syllabus – with Suggested Activities for each Specific Objective," a book especially designed for the mentally handicapped.

In assuming her new position, Cooke gave herself a mandate: to equip her students with the ability to master technology and manipulate information. To accomplish this, "teachers were charged to 'sell' their subjects to the students and parents or become redundant." She also wanted to educate parents on the importance of science to development and their role as parents in nurturing their children.

In addition to serving as a Vice-President and Treasurer of ISSA, Cooke served with distinction on several other ISSA committees. She also made notable contributions in the development of credit unions in the country.

In 2015, Cynthia Cooke was the recipient of the Order of Distinction from the Government of Jamaica "for service to Education."

There was the continuing problem of finding suitable teachers, particularly in the vocational and technical areas. To help alleviate the problem, the Embassy of Nigeria in Jamaica sponsored the establishment of The Technical Assistance Programme, under which Nigerian teachers are recruited by the Government of Nigeria to work in Jamaica in the fields of education and health for two years. Under the umbrella of this programme, two Nigerian teachers were engaged to teach History and Woodwork at Camperdown.

Despite the many challenges, Camperdown continued on its impressive growth path and teachers and students continued their outreach in many extra-curricular activities impacting community involvement and participation, such as volunteering at the Bellevue Hospital and at the Golden Age Home, as well as assisting at the Lincoln Kirk Basic School. Camperdown also participated in the Junior Achievement Programme sponsored by the Jamaica Chamber of Commerce, with the formation of a student-organized company, Kriss Kam Fashion, Ltd. Under this programme, private sector companies provided advisers in various areas of business to introduce students to different entrepreneurial activities, such as management, finance, marketing and production, in a novel introduction to the world of work. There was the Training Center that offered courses in personal hygiene, personal development and professional ethics, which offered a certificate in collaboration with the National Training Center. There was also the establishment of the Cosmetology Center to offer beauty services, hair care, skin care, facials, manicures and pedicures to staff and students.

It was during the nineties that Wavell Hinds came to national prominence with impressive performances in the schoolboy cricket competition. After outstanding displays with both bat and ball, Hinds received trophies for most centuries scored, best batting average, highest individual score, and with a bowling performance that included taking seven wickets in one match. Hinds was the recipient of the Michael Manley Award, as well as winning a $75,000 scholarship as the most outstanding batsman in the Sunlight Cup competition. He also captained the school in the Manning Cup.

Hinds served as captain of the Jamaica Youth cricket team and represented the West Indies Youth team. He later represented Jamaica and the West Indies senior teams in cricket. He played 45 test matches, 119 One-Day internationals, and 5 Twenty/20 matches for the West Indies. He made 5 test centuries and 14 half-centuries in tests, with a highest score of a double century (213). Hinds was the first recipient of the Courtney Walsh Award for Excellence, given in 2013.

At Boys' Champs (1998), Camperdown wins the Class 1 4x100m relay in a new record of 40.5s, and the Open 4x400m relay. David Spencer wins the Class 1 400m in 46.8s, becoming the first athlete in the history of Champs to run under 47s in the 400m. David Lloyd wins the Open 400m Hurdles in 52.2s.

Camperdown boys placed 7th in 1998; they finished in 8th position in 1999.

Camperdown continued its sprinting prowess at the Penn Relays in 1998. After placing 2nd in the 4x100m relay in 1997, in 1998 the team of Alix Rodriques, David Spencer, Damion Davis and David Lloyd wins in a time of 40.6 seconds. Surprising to many, it was the school's first win at the Penn Relays since 1989.

During this time, Camperdown remained competitive in other areas of sports, including male and female Basketball, Netball and Volleyball. By 1996,

THE STORY OF CAMPERDOWN HIGH SCHOOL

Camperdown wins the Under-14 Boys Basketball title: in 1997, the school is double Basketball champion – the Junior and the Senior League competitions. Two players, Mugabe Thomas and Richard Bailey, are selected to the U-19 national team for the Caricom tournament. By 1999, Thomas is the dominant player in the Schoolboys League, winning awards as Most Valuable Player in the Kentucky Fried Chicken All-Island Schoolboys Basketball Championships (1st in Shooting; 2nd in Rebounds; 2nd in Free Throws; 1st in Three-point shooting). Outstanding support comes from the other players, such as Rohan McKenzie, Michael Coleman, and Delano Mallott. Thomas was joined on that year's All-Star Schoolboys team by Coleman.

In 2007, the girls' track team places 8th at Champs, while the boys' finishes in 9th position. The school also sported a Rugby team and several members are invited to compete for the National team. In Track and Field, three students – Dagira Gordon (female), David Spencer, and Christopher McKenzie – win selection to represent Jamaica at the 1996 Carifta Games in Kingston, Jamaica. Spencer is one of the outstanding performers at the Games, winning two gold medals and one silver.

In football, Ricardo Fuller, a national Under-20 player, represented the senior team, the Reggae Boyz, before going on to a long and impressive run as a professional player in the English Premier League, one of the top football leagues in the world. Kevin King was a member of the Jamaica Under-17 team, and two students were members of the national Under-20, Under-17 and Under-16 teams.

The student population continued its steady growth and reached 1,394 by the mid-nineties. Accordingly, there are now 66 full-time teachers, two part-timers as well as one volunteer from Nigeria. In addition, there are 11 administrative and 19 ancillary staff members. Outstanding member of staff over many years, Vice-Principal Ralph Williams, left Camperdown to become Principal of Charlemont High School in St. Catherine. The period also witnessed a steady improvement in various academic disciplines, with outstanding results in science, especially in chemistry. Added to this is the fact that many graduates are winning places at the University of the West Indies and at the University of Technology, as well as at many overseas colleges and universities.

Additionally, many Camperdown students have won scholarships to American colleges and universities; many past students are now coaches at some of the most prominent American universities. Locally, Peter Cargill, Barrington Gaynor and Christopher Bender are named to the coaching staff of the national football programme.

Students continued to win several prizes in a number of extra-curricular activities, including gold medals in dancing, singing and drama festivals. Students Kadian Kellyman and Oral Hunter won several prizes in poster competitions. In 1997, Camperdown wins The Key Club Debating Competition, competed for amongst corporate area high schools. The school was national Chess champion for the 1997 season. Not to be outdone, 14-year old student, Robert Smith, is one of four Jamaican youngsters selected to travel to France as a Coco-Cola "ball boy' to participate at one of Jamaica's matches at the World Cup in 1998. In 2010, Shana Kay Cunningham is among the twelve Jamaican youngsters selected as a Coco-Cola "International Flagbearer" to participate in the World Cup in South Africa.

The Camperdown Steel Band also performed at the Inter-Schools Athletics Championships (Champs) and at a World Cup qualifying match at the National Stadium.

5

Forward Camperdown: The Journey Continues

Young Camperdown student, first former Karl Hazzard, was impressed to the point that he was challenged to express his youthful thoughts in poetry:

> We have **C**ourage in all difficulties.
> We have **A**mbition for the future.
> We have **M**ight!
> We have **P**ower!
> We have **E**nthusiasm for hard work:
> We have **R**ighteousness in our hearts.
> We never **D**esert our posts;
> We are **O**bedient to all above us
> We **W**ork without reward
> To build a **N**ation for tomorrow.

This and more too spells: **C-A-M-P-E-R-D-O-W-N**

The two decades spanning the end of the Twentieth Century and the beginning of the Twenty-First century found Camperdown in a period of sustained development and further growth, given the expansion in Jamaica's school-aged population. As new challenges and opportunities unfolded, the leadership of the school had little choice but to forge ahead despite the lack of adequate resources. The school's population continued to expand and by 2015 is 1,823. The academic, administrative and auxiliary staff component grow accordingly, totaling over 100 members. A similar situation exists throughout the country. This phenomenal growth in the country's high school student population comes about as more opportunities are created to expand secondary education to the ever-increasing number of eligible students in the country thirsting for meaning and opportunity, a remarkable change from earlier periods in the country's history when only the privileged few were able to gain access to secondary education.

To cope with the explosion in the high school population in the country, including those in Sixth Form, Camperdown, by now numbered among the leading high schools in the country, constructed a three-story building at a cost of J$10 million. By 2015, Camperdown's 6th Form catered to 300 students, an exponential increase from the six students who pioneered the school's first 6th Form in 1961. Provisions were also made in the curriculum for the new ROSE (Reform of Secondary Education) programme that was launched in 1993 by the Ministry of Education to rationalize the country's secondary education, particularly for grades seven through nine. At the same time, Chairman William McLeod also unveiled plans to construct an auditorium, much needed by the school, to provide an appropriate place for worship and other high-profile events.

Central to the ROSE programme were the following:

1. To provide equal access to quality education;
2. To enable Jamaican students to become productive citizens;
3. To achieve greater equity in the secondary school system to the grade 9 level; and
4. To improve the overall quality of education.

But the school continued to make strides. In 2001, student Leighton Brown was elected as District Governor for the Jamaica Key Club. During 2002, the school mourned the loss of teacher, Mrs. Dawn Marie Dacres-Shand.

In line with the changing academics, under the leadership of Physics teacher Mr. Kwanza Bailey, Camperdown in 2003 won the top prize and $30,000 for its entry, "Why Waste Waste," in the Energy Fair sponsored by the Jamaica Public Service Company. The winning entry was focused on generating electricity from sewage and solid waste. An additional prize of $15,000 was won for "the most innovative project," as well as a trophy for "being the most innovative and creative display."

But in order to cope with and manage the changing societal norms—the wanton disregard for discipline, law and order – and, as some would put it, "total disrespect and disregard for human life," new or alternate methods had to be implemented. The change in societal norms was among the new realities that the teachers and those charged with dealing with the nation's youth faced, in a constant and daily barrage. Back in the 1970s, Camperdown, like other high schools in a changing Jamaican landscape, had to live the reality of relentless changes. In 1984, for example, the school had to grapple with the situation whereby a young student, Kirk Johnson, who gained a place in the school through examination, was denied entry because of his dreadlock Rastafarian hairstyle. The case was settled in his favour by the Supreme Court.

Despite this initial setback, Johnson entered Camperdown and was very active in sports, representing the school in cricket, football, basketball and softball. He was also selected as a member of the country's Under-14 football team. Academically, he was successful with eight CXC passes, plus Additional Mathematics at the GCE Advanced Level. Johnson explained his Camperdown experience in a rather stoical way: "The thing about Camperdown is that it strengthened me in order to take criticism and prejudice" (***The Sunday Gleaner***, July 13, 1997).

The early years of the new century see Camperdown, like so many other institutions dealing with the nation's youth, being impacted negatively by the growing lack of respect for law and order and everyday regulations in society. To deal with this new phenomenon, the school developed a workable student manual, a sort of school contract, outlining rules and regulations spelling out lines of communications, deportment, punctuality, attendance, the proper and acceptable wearing of uniform, classroom cleanliness, homework assignments, search procedures, and prohibition of drugs and weapons, or contrabands on school premises. "Conduct yourself in such a manner," the student manual declares, "that your school and country will be proud of you."

There was the almost daily ritual of student fights and other anti-social activities, including murder, taking place on school campuses in the country. Camperdown was not immune to these wide societal problems. In

FORWARD CAMPERDOWN: THE JOURNEY CONTINUES

2006, Camperdown student, Jonhoi Vaughn, dedicated a poem to a fallen schoolmate, delivered at the Poetry Society of Jamaica fellowship at the Edna Manley College of the Visual and Performing Arts: "A schoolmate of mine from Camperdown was stabbed and killed," he wrote. "I tried to run, but I could not break free, for my hand the mirror clutched…there I stood, looking at my own reflection."

As a stark reminder of the crisis in the society, back in 1998, Mr. Abraham Lee, the school's watchmen for over ten years, was murdered on the school premises.

Over the years, there were several rotations in the school chaplaincy, which remains an integral part of the Camperdown experience. From Reverend Douglas Miller and Reverend Gladstone Donalds forward, several others have served in this fittingly appropriate position – Reverend Talmadge Ebanks, Reverend Yvette Noble-Bloomfield, Reverend Dave Hazle, Reverend Nigel Pusey, Reverend Garfield Vernon, Reverend Lorna Letts-Jones, and Reverend Nevroy Francis. The Camperdown family is ever grateful for their spirited participation in the life of the school.

The school included in its offerings a course in Ethics, one of two schools under the umbrella of the United Church to provide this. Reverend Dave Hazle and others, including Pastor Adrian McLean, taught the course in Ethics and assisted with guidance counselling. The school also mandated a moment of prayer at the end of each school day, continuing a norm from the earliest days. Remedial courses were instituted for students with grades lower than 70 percent in Mathematics and 60 percent in English to attend compulsory after-school classes to improve in these subjects. Mr. Anthony Garwood (past student) was made Vice-Principal in the Upper School and Mrs. Sophia Murray Vice-Principal in the Lower School. Murray later served as Vice-Principal in the Upper School when Garwood left to take up the position of Principal of the Charlie Smith High School, before moving on as Principal of the Dinthill Technical High School.

A number of other innovations were instituted as a way of improving the overall dynamics in the school, including the implementation in 2016-17 of a programme aimed at boosting the academic profile of the school. The programme, called "Mission Possible," the brainchild of teacher Mrs. Keniesha Brown-Russell, is an inspirational attempt to get all Camperdown students to pass at least five subjects at the CSEC (Caribbean Secondary Education

Certificate) level, as the school sought to re-culture its students to move above normalized mediocrity and aim for the highest, in a profoundly realistic attempt to live its motto.

By 2018, some 78% of those taking the CSEC examinations had passing grades in three or more subjects.

In a perpetuation of the normalized rigid social stratification system in the country, schools as Camperdown do not benefit from receiving the most outstanding students based on results from the annual Common Entrance Examination, despite closeness to the school of the community from where these students hail. Much of the school's intake of students each year show predominant numbers from under-served and depressed, tough urban communities wreaked by crime and violence, with commensurate low academic expectations. Situations as these result in difficult family life. Many students who attend Camperdown also travel across town from faraway communities, including Portmore in St. Catherine.

This is how one student, who went on to become a high-achieving student, remembers her situation back in 2018:

> My mom was my father, best friend and motivator, and she gave me the fuel to persevere. I could remember moments when my mom had to go to work for long hours, and the lunch she received at work became my dinner. There were moments when she had to do her clients' hair, and my grandma and I had to do without.

Despite this, the teachers and staff have never been daunted by this reality, and have laboured on – cajoling, inspiring, demanding, arguing, fussing—doing so with an inspirational twist that elicited the best from their charges. For many of the students, teachers were, in essence, "in loco parentis." At the same time, Camperdown's family atmosphere of care and regard for its students, nurturing and developing, continue to produce outstanding and successful students, as end results show. As a matter of fact, the staff take special pride in working hard to bring out the best talent and creative energies of the students who travel the Camperdown route. As such, much emphasis is placed on expressions of gratitude, respect for others, responsible citizenship, competence, the pursuit of excellence, despite the difficulties encountered and the odds that must be faced. It was, appropriately, the choir mistress who encouraged a young student to develop what in her view was a God-given talent. That young student, Neville Livingston (aka Bunny Wailer), went on to form, with Bob Marley and Peter Tosh, the world-famous Wailers Band. Many Camperdownians recall being bluntly told by their teachers that "life doesn't offer charity; it offers opportunities."

Back in 2002, student Leighton Brown expressed his thoughts this way: "Camperdown was a home and family for most of us. For many, it was a place where we could grow and dreams became a reality. Through these times at this institution, we have met friends who have touched our lives and whom we will remember forever."

This atmosphere of family inspired many parents to send their children to Camperdown, and it was not uncommon, year after year, to see siblings gracing the campus. In the eras of the 1930s through the 1950s, a very familiar sight would be the children of the teachers, such as the Grants, the MacPhersons, the Girvans, and the Harriotts. As the years rolled on, there were the Quarries from Harbour View (five brothers – Wilmot, Donald, Edward, Raymond, and Clifton); the four Taylor girls from nearby Lincoln Road (Sonia, Patricia, Beverley, and Jessica); the Taylors from Belmont Road (Barbara, Vivienne, and Barrington); the Pinnock sisters from Fernandez Avenue (Sandra, Jean, and Carol – plus cousin, Judith Lambert); the Warrens (Donald, Cynthia, Stanislaus, and Calvert); brothers Lennox and Patrick Aquart, sister Christina, plus cousin Rita Aquart; the Burgess girls (Patricia, Constance "Grace," and Pamela) the Heslop sisters (Donna and Michelle); brother and sister, Hugh and Elaine Gilchrist; sisters Marie and Joy Carty; the Smith brothers from Harbour View (Byron, Lloyd and Glen, plus cousin Evril Morrison). Then there was the Brown family – sisters Yvonne and Beverley, plus cousins Lorna and Maxine.

For many students, Camperdown's legacy in the ethos of a better Jamaica is cemented in words as preparation, confidence, honesty, work, struggle, character, simplicity, courtesy, modesty, cleanliness, service, enthusiasm, initiative, patience, cooperation, perseverance, and humility. This community of family continued through the years, with sisters and brothers and cousins following the tradition (the Brown siblings, Waldo (Head Boy – 1970-71) and Celia (Head Girl – 1971-72); the Thomases, Robert (Head Boy – 1972-73) and Angela (Head Girl – 1973-74); the Williams brothers, Kenneth and Carlton; the McLeans (Adrian, Megan, Charles, Peter, Paul, Janet); the Williams—Ralph and Ruth; the Fagan siblings (Kimberly, Richard, Khadean, and Jodi-Ann); and sisters Maxine and Marlene Dawkins, in a continuum to engage in the Camperdown spirit.

To outstanding girl athlete, Audrey Llewellyn-Hunter, teacher Cynthia Cooke was like "a mother to all of us students and would even take from her own pocket to buy things that we needed to participate." Llewellyn-Hunter won many medals for the school and for Jamaica at the junior and senior levels and was named to the Jamaica team for the 1984 Olympics. Apart from her all-round performances at Champs and the junior level, the story is told of Llewellyn-Hunter's prowess on the football pitch, adding that she was years ahead of the time when football would become a popular sport for females.

Many Camperdown athletes also remember that during the long period of dominance by Camperdown female athletes, they could always count on the encouragement and support from others (many non-C'downers), as Olympians Mr. Ray Harvey, Miss Vilma Charlton, and Mrs. Ruth Williams-Simpson (who also served on the school's faculty), plus Mr. Earl Bailey and past student Mr. Glen Mills.

There are teachers – many described by students as "phenomenal persons" – who performed yeoman service in bringing out the best and pushing students to live the school's motto: Only the Best is Good Enough! Aaliyah Watson, deputy Head Girl and winner of the Jeff Brown Scholarship for 2018, said as much:

> The teachers at Camperdown High School are simply the best. Their ability to care and nurture makes them heroes in every sense of the word. The impact of their sacrifices is far reaching as it is filled with much grace and love. Truth be told, with the combination of my mother, step-father, grandmother and my teachers by my side,

I was bound to be a success....I had many sleepless nights....I must say that it was all worth it. I sat 8 CSEC subjects (Spanish, English, Principles of Business, Principles of Accounts, Biology, Chemistry, Human and Social Biology and EDPM [Electronic Document Preparation and Management]) and I achieved 8 grade 1's (7 straight A profile). To add to my success, I topped the Caribbean in EDPM.

There are many other inspiring teachers who have served the institution, including Mr. Raphael Forbes (who left to become Principal of Trench Town Comprehensive High School), Mrs. Diane Mayne, Mr. D. K. Irons (who went on as Vice-Principal at Kingston Technical High School), Mr. Stanley Williams (Principal of Mannings High School), his brother, Mr. Ralph Williams (Principal of Charlemont High School), Mr. Waldo Brown, Mr. Anthony Garwood (Principal of Charlie Smith High School and later Principal of Dinthill Technical High School), Mrs. Shirley Simmonds (outstanding teacher of Business Education, who also served as Vice-Principal in the Upper School), Mrs. Winnifred Robinson (Vice-Principal in the Lower School), Mr. Dennis Webster (Dean of Students and later Vice-Principal in the lower school), Ms. Jennifer Reece, and Mr. Gladston Poole, affectionately referred to by students as "Sir Maximum," for his insistence on nothing but excellence.

In 2007, in a most fitting gesture of appreciation, the Alumni Association honoured three retired Vice-Principals (Mrs. Myrtle Kellier, Mrs Diane Mayne, and Mrs. Shirley Simmonds), and one retired teacher, Mr. Destinal Smalling, at a Banquet at the Hilton Kingston Hotel, saluting them for their "long and distinguished service to the school."

Student Cody Weir expressed his appreciation to his former Principal, Mrs. Cynthia Cooke, in poetry in 2017:

The sun rise in the morning, so do you.
The sun energizes me, so do you.
The sun brightens my day, so do you.
But you encourage, teach and help me to become
What I am today,
And that is why I appreciate you!

Past student, Dr. Barrington Murray, a successful Physician in Florida, remembers the exhortation he received from Principal Jeff Brown: "Make sure that you attain your greatest potential. Whatever you can do at this point do it now as this is the time in your life where you are going to set the stage for what is to come."

In 1989, graduation speaker, past student Mrs. Irene Walter, challenged the students to a springboard of excellence by announcing an annual trophy, accompanied with a monetary award, to any student who gained seven or more Grade 1 passes in the CXC (Caribbean Examinations Council) examination. Student Christopher Montgomery took up the challenge!

The following year, Montgomery's external examination results showed 8 distinctions: 7 at the CXC level and 1 at the Ordinary Level. He also obtained a pass in Computer Studies.

Then there is Tumekie Blackwood: apart from being captain of both the Manning Cup football team and the School Challenge Quiz team, Blackwood was the school's top achiever in the CSEC examinations, receiving Grade 1's in General Mathematics, Additional Mathematics, Chemistry, Information Technology, Technical Drawing and Human and Social Biology, and Grade 2's in English, Biology and Physics. In 2017, he gained four CAPE subjects – Pure Mathematics, Physics, Chemistry and Caribbean Studies.

There is also Shinell Cockett, who emerged as the school's top CSEC female student in 2019 with Nine 1s (Biology, Chemistry, English Language, French, Spanish, Food and Nutrition, Information Technology, Human and Social Biology, and Principles of Accounts). Sheamar White appears as the top CSEC male student with seven 1s—Mathematics, English Language, Physics, Information Technology, Human and Social Biology, Principles of Accounts, and Principles of Business. Other students are following suit.

These students are valiantly following in the footsteps of so many other "foundation" students of Camperdown who went on to success, despite great odds. Numbered among the many are Leila James Tomlinson, who was the first Black Jamaican woman to win a scholarship to England. Olive Dixon was one of the first Jamaican women to earn a medical degree from Howard University in the United States. Dr. Muriel Lowe Valentine was among the inaugural class to do medicine at the University College of the West Indies (now University of the West Indies). Dr. Julius Garvey, son of National Hero,

FORWARD CAMPERDOWN: THE JOURNEY CONTINUES

Marcus Garvey, became a prominent Cardiac-Thoracic Surgeon in New York. Dr. Viola Anderson, among the first Camperdown students to benefit from the acquisition of the first Biology and Chemistry labs in 1962, went on to earn a science degree at Howard University, and then pursued medicine at Downstate Medical Center in New York, before eventually opening practices in New York and in Houston, Texas. Dr. Hortense Daphney (Ruddock) Maylor, also an early beneficiary of the new science laboratory, went on to earn a science degree from Howard University, before earning her medical degree from the University of the West Indies and then opening a successful practice in New York City.

In academics as well as in sports, the school continued to present a fully-integrated and highly relevant programme catering to the changing needs and interests of its primary stakeholders – the students—and pushing them to achieve all they can. This is thanks, in part, to the "Mission Possible" initiative – changing course, changing lives, changing futures.

Based on a ranking of all Jamaican high schools by "Educate Jamaica" in which 50 percent or more of all students from a single school sitting the annual CSEC examinations obtain 5 or more subjects, including Mathematics and/or English, Camperdown was ranked at number 45 in 2016. In 2018, Camperdown moved up in rank to number 41, a small, yet encouraging, increase from 2016; by 2021, the school made further progress to number 35. The school board also continued on its goal in making Camperdown a "Centre of Excellence."

During 2007, the school benefitted from a visit by Dr. Hamadoun Toure, General Secretary of the International Telecommunications Union, to view the progress made at the school through the e-Learning Project.

Despite losing the service of the outstanding and long-serving Drama teacher, Mr. Carl Davis, Camperdown continued to excel in the fields of Drama and the Performing Arts. The Performing Arts have played a significant role in the school's history and Camperdown has been the proud recipient of many prestigious awards in the cultural areas, among them the George Goode Trophy for singing, and gold, silver and bronze medals in music, dance and drama. In the Jamaica Cultural Development Commission Festival Competition in 2009, Camperdown won a gold medal in Vocal Gospel, and four silver medals in Instrumental, Jamaican Folk Song, and Pan Music. After all, this is a school with a tradition that has produced outstanding performers as Patsy Ricketts, Derrick Williams, Sharon Woolery, Winston Bell, Carolyn Coolery, and Cyrene Tomlinson, once a leading actor in a series of local productions. Carl Davis, who joined the Camperdown staff in 1979, was honoured by the past students in 2014 with the Ivy Grant Award for Excellence for his devotion to the school.

Key players behind the music success include talented teachers as the distinguished Dr. George Goode, the founder and conductor of the famous Diocesan Choir, and others as Miss Kathleen Webster-McFarlane and Miss Lilieth Martell. In Creative Dancing, Mrs. Dianne Mayne remains embedded in the annals of Camperdown, and Miss June Watson played an important role with the Camperdown Dancers, who won several awards and staged many memorable performances in the annual Jamaica Festival Competitions.

In 2008, Camperdown student, Kaydian Jones, was named as "Miss Teen Jamaica."

In 2009, Camperdown was the National Schools Chess champion. With students Warren Cornwall, Damion Davy, Peter Thomas and Rayon Walters, the programme grew and excelled under the leadership of Teacher and Coach Mr. Equitable Brown (past student), who, as a student, was described as a "teenage sensation" in Chess. Brown represented Jamaica at the 37th World Chess Olympiad. The Chess team was the Corporate Area and national champion in 2010, cementing its place as one of the top high school chess teams in the country. The team of Dayvian Grant, Oshane Reid, Greg Johnson and Tewana Mellace won many awards – National Championship trophy as Best Corporate Team, Best Board One – Dayvian Grant; Best Board Four – Greg Johnson; and Most Valuable Player – Tewana Mellace, a second-former. Back in 2000, the school's Chess programme got a big boost from a visit by Mr. Maurice Ashley, an International Grand Master of Chess, a visit made possible through past student, Dr. Basil Bryan.

Led by Johnoi Vaughn, Ricardo Brooks and Michelle Williams, and coached by teacher Mr. Samuel Martin, the school was national Debate champion in 2007; in that same year, student Ricardo Brooks was selected as a member of Jamaica's team to England to engage in the debate on "Reparation."

FORWARD CAMPERDOWN: THE JOURNEY CONTINUES

Camperdown remained dominant among high schools in Cheerleading, winning several trophies and participating in various events throughout the island, including stirring performances before thousands at Champs in 2010, during the Centennial celebrations of the Championships which started in 1910.

The Cheerleading team also participated in an International Competition in Florida and placed 11th out of 40 countries, and 34th out of 78 in the All Star Division. They were also chosen to represented Jamaica at the finals of the Caribbean Cheerleading Championship.

All in all, the school not only coped with the changing times, but in fact had become even more dominant in different areas of scholastic life.

⁓∞⁓

Apart from the many changes in the curriculum to keep pace with a changing society, sports continued to be important in the school's profile. At the 2002 World Junior Championships in Athletics held in Jamaica, Camperdown students Winston Hutton and Orion Nicely were members of Jamaica's silver medal-winning 4x100m relay team.

Many Camperdown student-athletes continued to enjoy success at Champs and went on to represent the country at the Carifta Games and at other international youth athletic championships. Outstanding among them are Remaldo Rose, Rasheed Dwyer, Kimour Bruce, and Nicola Legister. Lorenza Johnson won gold medals at Champs in the Pole Vault in 2006 and 2007; David Lloyd the gold medal in the Open 400m Hurdles in 1998; Nickeava Wilson was 2nd in the girls' Long Jump at the Penn Relays and was also a Commonwealth Games representative; in the same year, Bernardo Brady represented Jamaica at the World Junior Championships in Canada. Christopher McKenzie won the Class 3 100/200m double at Champs in 1995. As a junior athlete, Rose would end as the most successful of the lot. In a storied high school career, he also won a gold medal as a member of Jamaica's 4x100m relay team at the World Junior championships in 2006.

Led by Coach Jermaine Shand, himself a past student, Camperdown was a double winner at the Penn Relays in 2006, first winning the 4x100m relay with the team of Kimour Bruce, Remaldo Rose, Rasheed Dwyer, and

THE STORY OF CAMPERDOWN HIGH SCHOOL

Jermaine Dawkins, in a new record time of 40.13s. In the 4x400m relay, the team of Sandor Pennicot, Remaldo Rose, Rasheed Dwyer, and Rayon Lawrence was also victorious; Dwain Bryden and Saibel Anderson were the alternates. It marked the first time that the school was returning to the winner's podium in the 4x400m in 21 years, last winning that race in 1985. Remaldo Rose's performance in both relays was so convincing that he was named as the Penn Relay's outstanding High School Boys' athlete for 2006, only the third Jamaican boys' high school athlete to win this award in the 42 years that Jamaican high schools were competing at the Penn Relays.

At the 2006 Carifta Games in Guadeloupe, Rose won the U-20 Men 100m.

In 2014, the school inaugurated a new house—Mills House (colour light blue)—named in honour of past student, Glen Mills. After relinquishing duties as Jamaica's National Coach, Mills went on to establish the internationally recognized Racers Track Club with some of the country's leading senior athletes, along with a steady stream of international athletes, who all want to benefit from the expert guidance of one of the most outstanding coach of sprinters.

The internationally recognized Camperdown Classics, dubbed "The Showcase of Sprinters," co-founded by Glen Mills and Cynthia Cooke in 2004, is now a principal feature in Jamaica's track and field calendar. It attracts the leading high school teams in the country, as well as leading senior athletes, many of whom choose the Camperdown Classics to start their season.

Mills is the only coach to place the top three finishers in an internationally-recognized sprinting event, when Usain Bolt, Yohan Blake, and Warren Weir, all from Mills' Racers Club, were the top three finishers in the Men 200m final at the London Olympics in 2012, indeed a phenomenal accomplishment. Twelve of Mills' charges have won medals at the Olympics or World Athletics Championships. Mills received the IAAF (International Association of Athletics Federations) Lifetime Achievement Award in 2012.

FORWARD CAMPERDOWN: THE JOURNEY CONTINUES

Girls' football is now an integral part of the sport agenda at Camperdown and the school remains dominant in basketball and volleyball, winning national championships in both. In 1997, the girls' Basketball team won several trophies, including the Schoolgirls' League, with Tamilla Murray named as the MVP in both the Women's and Schoolgirls' Basketball Leagues. In 2015, the school won the ISSA Urban Senior Schoolgirl Netball Competition. In 2019, Christeina Bryan was invited to the Jamaica Senior Netball team, after representing the national Under-21 team and serving as Captain of the national Under-16 team. Bryan also played on the national Basketball Under-25 team, along with schoolmate, Tessia Parker. Continuing on this progression of excellence, Rushelle Burton, recognized as the fastest freshman in NCAA (National Collegiate Athletic Association) history in the 100m hurdles, was a member of Jamaica's team to the IAAF World Championships in 2017, and Britany Anderson, who broke the national and world records in the U-20 100m hurdles, running 12.71s in 2019.

In a survey done by Sports Max in 2017, Camperdown was ranked as the second best-performing girls' high school in the country, based on the top four performances across nine disciplines in the 2016/17 academic year, comprising track and field, football, cricket, basketball, netball, volley ball, swimming, hockey, and table tennis.

In a continuum of the school's success in different activities, Camperdown in 2020 wins championship honours in high school debate, volleyball, the ISSA Boys' Southern Conference Basketball championship, and the All-Island U-19 Basketball competition.

In 2022, after a 16-year spell without success at the Penn Relays, under Coach Okeile Stewart, the Camperdown team of Rimando Thomas, Junior Harris, Jason Lewis, and Roshawn Clarke roared back to the victory podium, winning the Championship of America boys 4x100m relay in 40.13s.

In 2010, the school welcomes another change in leadership as Mrs. Cynthia Cooke is replaced by another past student, Mr. Valentine Bailey.

Bailey attended Camperdown between 1978-1985. He earned a Bachelor's degree and a Certificate in Teaching from the University of the

West Indies, before returning to join the staff at Camperdown in 1997, and subsequently serving as Vice-Principal.

The teaching staff remained competent and, by and large, has done a monumental job in molding students and showing them the WAY. The students are highly motivated and, despite numerous challenges in their daily lives, are coping. The school's Guidance Counsellors have been engaged in Family Life education and vocational advice to students and offer much-needed assistance in the filing of university applications. Overall, the Guidance Department continues to offer a variety of services aimed at helping to foster the moral and spiritual development of their charges and instilling in them a care and concern for the underprivileged in the society.

Seminars are also held for parents and students, with relevant topics as "Effective Parenting," "Strategies for Effective Study," "Appropriate Conduct and Dress," and "Sexuality," all done to enhance the effectiveness of the school environment.

A dynamic society demands important changes and innovative experiences to affect values and behaviour. Camperdown, in this, is a natural leader. Though not generally seen as one of the top performing high schools in the country, it is not at the bottom either. According to former Principal Cynthia Cooke, Camperdown is a typical high school in the Jamaican landscape. To boost school spirit and community interest, there are events, such as "The Camperdown Walk," an annual Ethics Retreat, an annual "Evening of Excellence" to highlight students' performances, the annual Parents' Day, and the annual Founder's Day. But Camperdown is much more: not only concerned with mere certification, but to expand its horizon to satisfy stakeholders and the multiple educational and societal needs of the country.

The extra-curricular and enhanced programmes in place are wide-ranging and serve to support the academic curriculum, while nurturing students' overall development and leadership potential. These involve participation in School Challenge Quiz, 4-H, Key Club, The Red Cross Society, Science Club, Inter-Schools Christian Fellowship, Girls' Guide, Cadet Corps, Teen for Technology, Mathematics, National Spanish Quiz, Modern Languages, Reading Club, African Studies Club, Badminton, National Drama Festival, Fashion and Design, Junior Achievement Programme, Environment Club, I.C.W.I. (Insurance Company of the West Indies) Safety Week Exhibition, Art and Craft Poster Essay Competition, Literary and Debating Society,

FORWARD CAMPERDOWN: THE JOURNEY CONTINUES

CASI – Camperdown Association of Social Intervention, Steel Band, participation in annual Festival competitions organized by the Jamaica Cultural Development Commission, Music, Dance, Drama, and various other activities that enlighten and command the students' interests.

Students earn additional credits for participation in extra-curricular activities.

Responding to the ever-growing calls for assistance, past students have intensified their support to the alma mater and their relationship with the past students associations. They identify with the school's success in sports and in a wide range of other activities. They invest in the school's success and such success becomes embedded in their personal identity. From as early as the 1930s, past students have been making financial and in-kind contributions to the alma mater. From computers to sports gear to academic tools to financial support in welfare and scholarship initiatives, the support has grown exponentially to augment perennial short-falls in government funding. The message was simple: Though separated by distance and time, they (the past students) are still bonded by a deep love of alma mater and friendships formed.

The New York Chapter of the Past Students' Association was founded in 1992 to "foster friendship, goodwill, and support to the school" by a group consisting of Patrick Payne (President), Sonia (Jones) Clarke, Lois (Stewart) Anderson, Pauline (Morrison) Jones, Hermine (Taylor) Huie, Jeanette (Lightbourne) Gardner, Ena (Morrison) Madhere, and Rose (Thomas) Williams.

At the inaugural luncheon held in Long Island, New York, four teachers from the early years of the "new" Camperdown were honoured – Professor Oscar Harriott, Mrs. Isobel MacPherson, Mrs. Winifred Smith, and Mr. Raphael Forbes.

Others who have taken up the mantle of leadership and support in the New York area are Waldo Brown, Valerie (Johnson) Owen, Marlene Hobson, Beverly Blake, and Anthony Drummond.

THE STORY OF CAMPERDOWN HIGH SCHOOL

The Florida chapter (CASFLO) was re-organized in 2002 by an all-female group of past students comprised of Faith Simpson (President), Andrea Beckford Brown, Carol Burgess, Antoinette Grant-Palmer, Andrea Lyseight-Melbourne, Jennifer McLaren, Michelle Morell-Edwards, Gwendolyn Powell Miles, and Avery Williams-Lewis. Leadership of the chapter has also been held by Michelle (Chue-Sang) Cooper and Allan Cunningham, with strong support from others as Trevor Chambers, Robin Richards, Dawn Stimpson, Aston McKenzie, and Susaye Small. Over the years the chapter has committed millions of dollars to the school for general and student support and scholarships, including support to enable graduates to pursue tertiary education.

Since the 1930s, in every decade of the school's existence, past students have bonded to assist the school, raising funds for a variety of purposes. Over the years, many of these efforts endured periods of ebb and flow. In 2010, in yet another effort to "rally the troops," the Camperdown Alumni St. Andrew (Jamaica) chapter (CASTAC) was organized by a group that included Dennis Gordon, Peter Ruddock, William Watson, Claire Forrester, Joan McLeggon, and Rainford Wint. It sponsors a special Labor Day project, as well as an annual Health and Wellness Fair, with past students, particularly those in the medical and health science professions, donating time and resources to the welfare of the Camperdown community. Under the influence of past student Claire Forrester, CASTAC in 2012 also developed the "Adopt-A-Child" programme to assist the most vulnerable students at the school. The "Adopt-A-Child" programme calls upon alumni, friends of the school and well-wishers to reach out and give back to the molding and development of young lives.

A structured support system for sports comes through the work of CAMPSEC (Camperdown Sports and Extra-Curricular Committee), organized in 2016 to add extra impetus to the drive to provide increased alumni support and to engage in the management of extra-curricular activities. For many students who attend the school the need for everyday support is pressing. It is a good barometer of the direction of the country as many students need assistance with everyday basics as lunch money, books, uniforms, examination fees, and many other needs that some in the society take for granted.

The St. Andrew Chapter established the Camperdown "Hall of Fame" in 2011 to "showcase the best of our alma mater" and to recognize alumni who have excelled in their chosen fields. There is also the Ivy May Grant Award for

FORWARD CAMPERDOWN: THE JOURNEY CONTINUES

Excellence, given in recognition of outstanding contributions to the development of the school, and the Jeff Brown Award for Excellence in History, to recognize "Jeff" Brown, who guided the school through many successes and touched many young lives.

In 2010, the Ivy May Grant Scholarship Trust Fund was established.

Taken together, the alumni groups have donated millions of dollars in the continuous quest to assist the school.

Back in 1969, Ivy Grant communicated from New York by letter (dated February 6, 1969) with Mr. Ferdie Sangster, then Chairman of the school board, about the institutionalization of Adult Literacy classes for the community, in which Camperdown would play a leading role: "…If these can be continued," she wrote, "you will have the nucleus of a tremendous opportunity to serve the community and to appeal to Government for a cause closely affecting and strongly urging the support of the entire eastern Kingston."

It was Ivy Grant's passion that Camperdown would become a place where social class and financial standing would not be important in determining one's desire to better oneself and become educated.

Ivy Grant always dreamt of Camperdown growing from a small preparatory school to a position of great influence in the community that it calls home – the enduring Biblical lesson of the acorn and the oak—serving that community, giving hope, and involving it in personal and community development. In an early interview, she expressed the trust that "the foundation of the stately pile that is now Camperdown High School," was built by those who "toiled with body, mind and soul to light a beacon of Christian Education in Eastern Kingston that would shed its rays in every region from which the school's population was gathered." It was her hope that "Camperdown, under God's guidance to the school's dedicated Principal and Staff, will continue to give to our nation men and women of Christian worth and noble achievements."

In 2004, in the aftermath of Hurricane Ivan, Camperdown students journeyed to the Portland Cottage All-Age School in Clarendon to assist the local branch of the Red Cross in volunteer service, singing songs, and offering hope to those in need.

From Ivy Grant, to Jeff Brown, to Winifred Smith, to Cynthia Cooke, to Valentine Bailey, the leadership and staff of Camperdown fully embody the school's intrinsic goal: "To build up self-esteem among the students and to inculcate values that will enhance personhood; never forget[ting] that those you teach are our potential leaders – the people who represent the kind of future we are likely to have as a nation."

And in keeping with that vision of charity, peace, and love, each school day at Camperdown ends in a moment of prayer.

Ivy Grant's dream is everyday being carried out in countless ways. The little "home school" has fulfilled this dream. Camperdown today counts among its many graduates those who have risen to national and international fame – professors, engineers, scholars, doctors, dentists, nurses, police/security officers, university administrators, principals and teachers, public servants, judges, lawyers, entrepreneurs and innovators, athletes, entertainers and musicians – professionals all, in the wide range of disciplines that bring pride and joy to the society.

Despite the lack of any infrastructure for proper training or the playing of games on the school's premises on Camperdown Road, yet the school can proudly boast among its extraordinary contributions to the international profile of Jamaica, some of the most accomplished athletes the country has produced. Donald Quarrie was the first Jamaican to win an Olympic gold medal in sprinting and, in the 1970s, was recognized as the best 100/200m runner in the world. Raymond Stewart is the first sprinter in history to make three consecutive Olympics 100m finals. In the World Track and Field Athletics Championships in 1987, Stewart and Andrew Smith won bronze medals in the 4x100m relay, the very first time that Jamaica was winning a relay medal at these games. And back in 1986, three Camperdown past

FORWARD CAMPERDOWN: THE JOURNEY CONTINUES

students (Raymond Stewart, Andrew Smith, and Leroy Reid) comprised three-quarters of Jamaica's 4x100m team that won the silver medal at the Central American and Caribbean Games in Santo Domingo, Dominican Republic.

Ronetta Smith won a bronze medal as a member of Jamaica's 4x400m team at the 2004 Olympics in Athens. She also won a silver medal at the World Championships in 2005 (4x400m), and a bronze medal (4x400m) in the 2003 World Championships. At the 1996 Olympics in Atlanta, Andria Lloyd won a bronze medal as a member of Jamaica's 4x100m team.

Rasheed Dwyer won a gold medal in the 200m at the Commonwealth Games in 2014; a gold medal (4x200m) at the IAAF World Relays in 2014; and a gold medal (4x100m) at the World Athletics Championships in 2015.

Music: Neville Livingston (Bunny Wailer) is a founding member (with Bob Marley and Peter Tosh) of the international music band, The Wailers. Known as "Bunny" by all his friends from Camperdown days, Bunny Wailer played a stellar role in pioneering Reggae music nationally and internationally. He is the writer of "Electric Boogie," the song that sparked an international dance craze. Bunny Wailer is also the winner of three Grammy Awards (1991, 1995, 1997), one of the highest-profiled winners of the vaunted award; Hopeton Lewis recorded the highly successful No. 1 hit, "Take it Easy," and is credited as the originator of the Rock Steady beat. In 1970, Lewis was also winner of the annual National Festival Song Competition with his hit song, "Boom Shaka Laka." In 1992, Heather Grant became the first female winner in the 27 years of the competition with her song, "Meck Wi Put Things Right." Back in 1990, she was the lead singer on the hit song, "Workie Workie," with the Byron Lee and the Dragonnaires band.

Another Camperdownian, Althea Hewitt, enjoyed an impressive hit with "Love that a Woman Should Give to a Man," from her debut album in 2008. Vernon Edwards is the recipient of the Lifetime Achievement Award, presented in 2008 by the Vinyl Record Collectors Association, to recognize those "who share a passion for vinyl music." Other past students who have made a big impact on the society include internationally recognized entertainers Wayne Wonder (Von Wayne Charles), Spragga Benz (Carlton Grant), Assassin (Jeffrey Campbell), and Baby Cham (Damian Beckett). Another past student, Desmond Young, gave distinguished service as President of the Jamaica Federation of Musicians from 1995 to 2017. Apart from being lead vocalist for the popular Caribs band, Young was also a finalist in the annual Festival Song competition in 1973.

Football: Peter Cargill was Vice Captain of the "Reggae Boyz," the history-making Jamaica national football team that was the third from the Caribbean, but the first English-speaking Caribbean country, to reach football's World Cup Finals in 1998. Camperdown has placed numerous players on the national football teams (at all levels). Peter Cargill and Ricardo Fuller are among the few players born in Jamaica to play top-flight international football (Cargill in Israel and Fuller in the English Premier League).

Cricket: several past students have represented Jamaica at different levels. Wavell Hinds, apart from representing the West Indies in cricket, also served as President of the West Indies Players Association.

Public Service: During the 1970s, Louis Lindsay served as an Advisor to the Prime Minister of Jamaica and as Permanent Secretary in the Ministry of Local Government and Community Development; Ambassador Marjorie Taylor served as Senator in the Jamaican Senate and as Minister of State for Labour, Welfare and Sports. In 1992, she was elected as Member of Parliament for the East Kingston and Port Royal constituency. She also served as the country's Ambassador for Children; Ambassador Dr. Basil Bryan, University Lecturer, Author and Diplomat, has the distinction as the longest-serving Consul General of Jamaica in New York, serving in the post for 10 years; Devon Rowe is among the select few Jamaicans to serve as the country's Financial Secretary, the highest financial position in the Public Service; and Jackie Lucie-Smith gave many dedicated years as a Public Servant, rising to the highest level in the Ministry of Education.

Coaching: Glen Lebert Livingstone Mills ranks among an elite band of history's greatest Track and Field coaches. He is responsible for guiding Usain Bolt to 8 Olympics and 11 World Championships gold medals, and world records in the 100m (9.58s), the 200m (19.19s), and the 4x100m relay (36.84s).

Above all, Camperdown is the only Jamaican high school to have both

FORWARD CAMPERDOWN: THE JOURNEY CONTINUES

girls' and boys' track teams (in 1997 and 2003, respectively) enshrined on the prestigious Penn Relays' "Wall of Fame."

Camperdown's contributions to Jamaica are countless!

Ivy Grant's dream lives in the numerous men and women (the boys and girls) who rose from the small grounds of Camperdown High School to become nation-builders, focused on the task with gusto, character, and dignity.

The early years of Camperdown were pregnant with hope and determination. In those trying periods it was uncertain where the road would lead. Camperdown today remains a living demonstration of the unconquerable will of the people, even those from less privileged circumstances, to succeed despite the obstacles.

Ninety-two years after a very modest start, Ivy Grant's dream lives on!

The extraordinary purpose of Camperdown is nicely captured in this poem written by a young student, Rohan Facey:

I have seen days when the winds rattled at my windows and huffed and puffed at my existence.
I have seen days when torrential rains tried to attack and smear my reputation.
But I was born resilient, and unstoppable has always been in my eyes.
I am a **DIAMOND IN THE EAST**,
Scoffed at, laughed at, battered,
Taken for granted, but still I tower
Above the dirt that has been used against me.
I am ripe with age and history.

THE STORY OF CAMPERDOWN HIGH SCHOOL

Smug,
Counting the success stories of my children.
For, my children are lawyers, doctors, principals,
Vice principals, teachers, nurses, sporting giants;
In fact, they have touched the world
In every good profession under heaven!
Yes, like Maya Angelou –
I rose from the ash of insignificance to sit on the front page of history.
Like Mandela –
I smashed prejudice and stigma to show that I too can lead the way
to greatness.

"Only my best is good enough."
I am Camperdown…

….charged to tell Camperdown's story in words and deeds – everyday, everywhere, to everyone – to let all know that diamonds, too, are made in the East.

Pictorial Journey (1960s forward)

[Courtesy of Camperdown High School]
The family house on the property of #6B Camperdown Road (front view) becomes the main building of the 'new' Camperdown High School (1958)

THE STORY OF CAMPERDOWN HIGH SCHOOL

[Courtesy of Camperdown High School]
This building (side view) housed the Principal's office, library, staff room for teachers, a sick room, and a number of classrooms. A few classrooms were constructed in other areas of the premises, including an 'open' classroom that also provided an assembly space for morning devotion.

[Courtesy of Camperdown High School]
This building housed several classrooms

PICTORIAL JOURNEY (1960s FORWARD)

[Courtesy of Camperdown High School]
Prizegiving (1959) – student Jean Pinnock receiving trophy for academic excellence.
(left to right) Reverend Douglas Miller, Mrs. Florizel Glasspole (wife of the Member of Parliament), Mr. Noel White (Acting Principal).
[Note: uniform is dark tunic (cocoa brown) with beret and white blouse]

THE STORY OF CAMPERDOWN HIGH SCHOOL

[Courtesy of Camperdown High School]
Groundbreaking for new building (January 1960) watched by students (left to right) Reverend Douglas Miller (Chairman of the School Board); Mr. F. L. Sangster (with shovel); Reverend Gladstone Donalds; Mr. Noel White (Acting Principal).

[Courtesy of Camperdown High School]
First new building (1961)

PICTORIAL JOURNEY (1960s FORWARD)

[Courtesy of Camperdown High School]
Another new building (1964)

[Courtesy of Camperdown High School]
Sports day at school premises—#6B Camperdown Road (1961). High Jump and Long Jump took place the day before moving over to Kensington Park where the races were held. Teacher Mr. Raphael Forbes is in necktie.

THE STORY OF CAMPERDOWN HIGH SCHOOL

[Courtesy of Camperdown High School]
   Class Picture (1961); Note ratio of girls to boys

[Courtesy of Camperdown High School]
   Class picture (1961)
Form Teacher Mrs. McPherson is seated center between Prefects Lascelles Williamson and Sylvia Anderson
[Note: 30 students in class – 27 girls and 3 boys]

PICTORIAL JOURNEY (1960s FORWARD)

[Courtesy of Camperdown High School]
Class picture (1962)
With senior students (standing left) Eleanor Sparkes,
(standing right) Dorothy Mitchell

[Courtesy of Camperdown High School]
Class Picture (1962)
Students with Prefect Beverly Randall (standing far right) and Prefect
Sandra Pinnock (stooping far right), Form Mistress Grace Sinclair is
standing 3rd left.
[Note: Ratio of girls to boys; beret as part of girl's uniform]

[Courtesy of Sandra Pinnock Wiley]
Latin Teacher and Form Master, Mr. Keith King (Form 5B2) with students (1962)
(L) Joy Sang and (R) Joyce Gangadeen
[Note: dark brown uniform with white blouse]

PICTORIAL JOURNEY (1960s FORWARD)

[Courtesy of Camperdown High School]
History Club educational trip (1963)
(back row left to right), Dorothy Mitchell, Lorna Brown, Jean Pinnock, Joyce Gangadeen (middle row left to right) Patricia Taylor, Sandra Pinnock, Mrs. Myrtle Burke (Club Advisor) and Yvonne Pinnock (stooping left to right) Marcia Thomas and Trevor Myers (HB,1962-63)

THE STORY OF CAMPERDOWN HIGH SCHOOL

[Courtesy of Camperdown High School]
Student Viola Anderson accepts prize for academic work (1964) [Note: change in uniform]

[Courtesy of Olga Marston]
Student Olga 'Bibby' Marston models new school uniform (1964) [Note: change in uniform includes addition of straw hat instead of beret]

PICTORIAL JOURNEY (1960s FORWARD)

[Courtesy of Camperdown High School]
Softball Team (1964) – (kneeling left to right) Maxine Brown, Ann Smith, Winsome Wright, Olga Marston;
(standing left to right) Mr. Roy Archer (Coach), Carol Pinnock, Viola Anderson, Shirley Lynch, Camille Orridge, Roberta Thompson, Mr. George Aboud (Asst. Coach).

[Courtesy of Camperdown High School]
Michael Murray (1966) one of the most accomplished sprint/hurdlers to compete at Champs

THE STORY OF CAMPERDOWN HIGH SCHOOL

[Courtesy of Barrington Taylor]
Camperdown's first appearance in the Penn Relays (1966)
(left to right) Michael Murray; Llewellyn Facey; Barrington Taylor;
Anthony Attride

[Courtesy of Hewitt Depass]
Jamaica All-Schools Track and Field Team (1966) before leaving on tour of Eastern Caribbean.
Three Camperdown students selected:
kneeling second from right is Donald Quarrie, kneeling third from right is Anthony Attride;
standing sixth from left is Michael Murray.

PICTORIAL JOURNEY (1960s FORWARD)

[Courtesy of The Gleaner Co.]
Class 2 Stars: Donald Quarrie (centre) and Godfrey Murray (right) of Camperdown get a helping hand from their assistant coach Dennis Dixon after they placed first and second, respectively, in the 100 yards at Champs on Saturday, March 18, 1967

[Courtesy of Camperdown High School]
Penn Relays Team (1968)
(left to right) Rupert McCleary, Godfrey Murray, Hugh Taffe, Deputy Headmaster Raphael Forbes, Headmistress Ivy Grant, Donald Quarrie, Winston Hobson and Patrick Minzie

[Courtesy of Bryan Family Collection]
(left to right) Mrs. Winifred Smith, Mrs. Ivy Grant, Mr. Henry Mc D. Messam at wedding of past students, Basil Bryan and Jean Pinnock, Kingston Sheraton Hotel (1969)

PICTORIAL JOURNEY (1960s FORWARD)

[Courtesy of Eric Barrett]
Penn Relays (1971)—Taken shortly after Camperdown's 2nd Place finish in 4x100m
(left to right) Donovan Russell, Eric Barrett, Patrick Minzie and Edward Quarrie
Standing (far right) – Everton Powell – a member of the 4x400m team

[Courtesy of Camperdown High School]
Coach Glen Mills (circa 1970s)

THE STORY OF CAMPERDOWN HIGH SCHOOL

[Courtesy of Camperdown High School]
Choir in performance at school event (circa 1970s)
At piano is member of staff, Angela Fortella, also a past student

[Courtesy of Camperdown High School]
Inspection of Cadet Corps (circa 1970s)

PICTORIAL JOURNEY (1960s FORWARD)

[Courtesy of Camperdown High School]
  Day School class picture (circa 1970s)

[Courtesy of Camperdown High School]
  Extension School class picture (circa 1970s)

THE STORY OF CAMPERDOWN HIGH SCHOOL

[Courtesy of Camperdown High School]
  Mrs. Ivy Grant and Olympian Donald Quarrie
  in embrace celebrating Quarrie's gold and silver medals won
  in 1976 Olympics in Montreal, Canada

PICTORIAL JOURNEY (1960s FORWARD)

[Courtesy of The Gleaner Co.]
CHAMPIONS—Members of the Camperdown High School team who won the Tappin Knock-Out Cricket final by scoring an easy nine-wicket victory over Kingston Technical School at Kensington Park on July 6, 1978).
Sitting (L-R) are Dennis Gordon, Adrian Faulkner, Earl Melbourne (capt.), Patrick Dawes and Donald Davidson. Standing (L-R) are Lloyd Morgan (coach), Percy Tomlinson, Thomas McLean, Wayne Stoddart, Seiveright Meggoe, Carlton Williams, Dave Harris, Michael Deans, Donald Morrison, Errol Taylor, Astley Crawford and Mr. Jeff Brown, Headmaster.

THE STORY OF CAMPERDOWN HIGH SCHOOL

[Courtesy of Camperdown High School]
Choir in performance at Prizegiving (1978)

[Courtesy of Camperdown High School]
MANNING CUP AND OLIVIER SHIELD CHAMPIONS (1978): (Standing L – R) Coach Jackie Walters, Ronald Headlam, Wayne James, Donovan Lambert, Ripton White, Delroy Lewis, Anthony Lewis, Errol Blake, Principal Jeff Brown, (Sitting L – R) Eric Maynard, Samuel Duncan, Barrington Edwards, Kenneth Henry, Wayne Williams, (In Front L – R) Kevin Purrier, Carlton Williams, Thomas McLean, Lloyd Crawford

PICTORIAL JOURNEY (1960s FORWARD)

[Courtesy of The Gleaner Co.]
MANNING CUP AND OLIVIER SHIELD FOOTBALL CHAMPIONS FOR A SECOND YEAR RUNNING WITH THEIR COACH AND HEADMASTER (1979):
(stooping in front, left to right): Donovan Corcho, Errol Blake, Carlton Williams, Kenneth Henry (vice captain), Peter Cargill and Patrick Dawes; (middle row, left to right): Peter Trail, Gladstone Heron, Errol Myrie, Coach Jackie Walters, Everton Grant, Richard Gordon, Richard Green; (back row, left to right): Peter Hibbert, Ronald Headlam, Dean Davidson, Michael Brown, Headmaster Geoff Brown, Eric Maynard, Delroy Lewis, Mark Salmon and Lloyd Crawford

THE STORY OF CAMPERDOWN HIGH SCHOOL

[Courtesy of Camperdown High School]
Camperdown Netballers (circa 1980's)

[Courtesy of Camperdown High School]
*Record-breaking 4x100m team after victory at Penn Relays (1981)
(left to right) Oswald Cole, Leroy Reid, Headmaster Jeff Brown, Wayne Morrison and Howard Lawrence*

PICTORIAL JOURNEY (1960s FORWARD)

[Courtesy of Camperdown High School]
Triple Crown Champions (1982)
(standing left to right) Ricardo Hyde, Steve Nelson, Richard Green, Christopher Bender, Carl Herbert, Andrew Hines, Peter Cargill, Mark Salmon and Carl Richards
(kneeling left to right) Prince Topey, Nyron Prawl, Claude Palmer, George Malcom, Dale Palmer, Winston Campbell. Barrington Gaynor and Michael Clark

THE STORY OF CAMPERDOWN HIGH SCHOOL

[Courtesy of Camperdown High School]
Girls Track Team (circa 1989)
(Standing left) Coach Raymond KC Graham
Andria Lloyd (front row 5th from left) won bronze medal (4x100m relay) in 1996 Olympic Games in Atlanta, Georgia

[Courtesy of Camperdown High School]
Award-winning Camperdown Dancers in performance (circa 1980's)

PICTORIAL JOURNEY (1960s FORWARD)

[Courtesy of Camperdown High School]
Noted Soprano, past student Carole Reid, in performance at fundraising concert for Camperdown High School (1989)

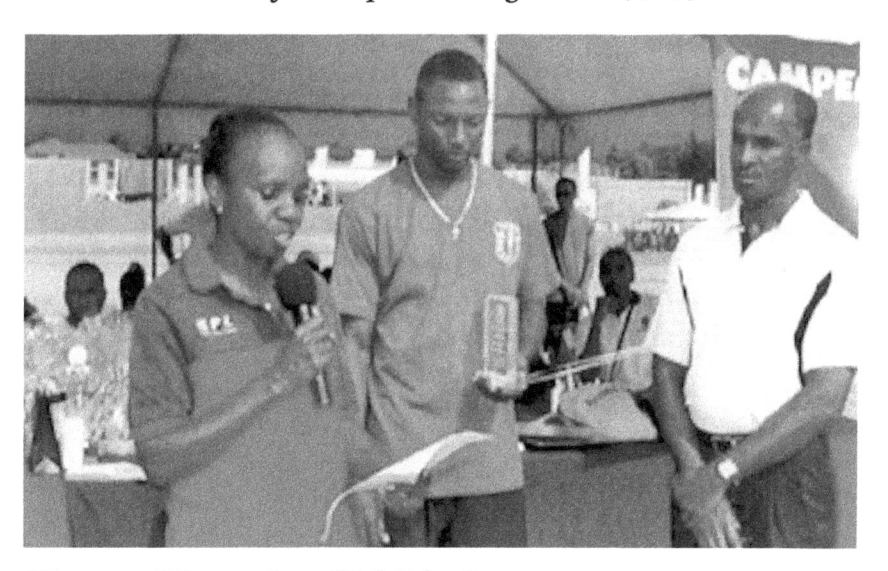

[Courtesy of Camperdown High School]
Cynthia Cooke, Rasheed Dwyer and Donald Quarrie at Camperdown Classics (2006)

[Courtesy of Bryan Family Collection)
Penn Relays (2006) – Record breaking 4x100m team
(left to right) Past Student Mrs. Jean Bryan, Coach, Remaldo Rose,
Kimour Bruce, Jermaine Dawkins, Rasheed Dwyer, and Past Student
Dr. Basil Bryan

PICTORIAL JOURNEY (1960s FORWARD)

[Courtesy of The Daily Gleaner]
Under-14 National Champions (2007)
Members of Camperdown Under-14 Football Team after winning Malta/ISSA Under-14 Title,
defeating St. James High School 2-1

[Courtesy of Camperdown High School]
Members of hard-working Canteen staff

THE STORY OF CAMPERDOWN HIGH SCHOOL

[Courtesy of Vivienne Taylor Fullerton]
"Give Back Day" (2019)
Past students (Florida Chapter) with award-winning students

[Courtesy of Marcia Moo Young]
All-Island champion Basketball Team (2019) with mentor, Past Student
Mrs. Marcia Moo Young

PICTORIAL JOURNEY (1960s FORWARD)

[Courtesy of Boris Robinson]
Past students Everald Fletcher and Boris Robinson at annual Reunion Gala (2020)

THE STORY OF CAMPERDOWN HIGH SCHOOL

[Courtesy of Boris Robinson]
Past students Desmond Young and (Bunny Wailer) Neville Livingston at annual Reunion Gala (2020)

PICTORIAL JOURNEY (1960s FORWARD)

[Courtesy of Camperdown High School]
End of term class picture

[Courtesy of Camperdown High School]
Junior students celebrate end of school year and beginning of holidays

THE STORY OF CAMPERDOWN HIGH SCHOOL

[Courtesy of Camperdown High School]
Champion Netball / Track Athletes

PICTORIAL JOURNEY (1960s FORWARD)

[Courtesy of Camperdown High School]
Manning Cup and Olivier Shield Champions (1979)
(back left to right) Mr. Jeff Brown (Principal), Eric Maynard, Michael Brown, Delroy Lewis, Lloyd Crawford, Peter Hibbert and Jackie Walters (Coach)
(middle left to right) Dean Davidson, Richard Gordon, Everton Grant, Errol Myrie and Gladstone Heron
(front left to right) Peter Cargill, Peter Trail, Kenneth Henry (Vice Captain), Carlton Williams (Captain) and Errol Blake

Not in Picture – Donovan Corcho, Patrick Dawes and Mark Salmon

Appendix 1a

CAMPERDOWN HIGH SCHOOL
16½ PORTLAND ROAD, KINGSTON, JAMAICA.

PROSPECTUS
ONLY THE BEST IS GOOD ENOUGH.

1947

Appendix 1b

Aim
The School gives kindly, individual attention to all pupils and its aim is to prepare them for practical, efficient, Christian living.

Admission
Pupils, both boys and girls, can enter the Kindergarten Department, at four years of age. The Preparatory Department accepts pupils between the ages of seven and twelve years. In the High School Department ONLY GIRLS are admitted as pupils.

There is no special entrance examination other than that for deciding the form to which the pupil shall be assigned. In the case of pupils from another school, a Certificate of Conduct is required from the former Principal and must accompany the Form of Application correctly filled out, dated and signed by the applicant's parents. Parents must vouchsafe children's good health upon admission.

The Principal may find it necessary to require the withdrawal of pupils or to suspend their attendance for persistent idleness, disobedience or any serious misconduct. In every other instance, notice of withdrawal of a pupil must be received by the Principal by the Opening Day of the New Term in which the pupil is in attendance at School, or a full Term's fee must be paid in lieu of such notice.

Curriculum
Pupils are prepared for the London Matriculation, the Local Examinations of the University of Cambridge, Junior and School Certificate and the Examinations of the Royal Associated Board of Music.

The regular school curriculum includes: Reading, Writing, Religious Knowledge, English, History, Latin, Spanish, Arithmetic, Algebra, Geometry, Geography, Nature-Study, Hygiene and Physiology, Drawing and Painting, Physical Training with National Dancing, Class-Singing and Needlework.

HOUSEHOLD ECONOMICS
Plans are being made to erect a kitchen where classes in Elementary Cookery, Table-Setting, Service and Decoration will be conducted.

CLASS SINGING
The girls of the Upper School are taught vocal music by Mr. G. D. Goode, I.S.O., who is the visiting Instructor in that subject.

Appendix 1c

Fees

(Library and Games Fees are Included)

	£ s. d.	
Children under the age of 7	...	per term
Children between 7 and 12 years	...	"
Girls over 12 years	...	"
Music (extra, Piano and Theory)	...	"
Percussion Band (extra)	...	"

N.B. No student will be admitted to classes without a registration card which is issued upon the payment of the full Term's Fees on registration day prior to re-opening.

A full Term's Notice or a full Term's Fee in lieu thereof is required before the withdrawal of any pupil.

All Fees are non-returnable, even if a pupil is withdrawn, suspended or expelled.

There will be no reduction of fees for two or more children attending school from the same family.

The Principal will be pleased to see parents on any day by appointment. All letters relating to pupils or business matters should be addressed to the Principal, NOT to any member of the staff.

Attendance and Hours

The School Year consists of three terms: The Easter term, January to Holy Week; the Summer term, April to July; and the Christmas term, September to December.

School hours are from 8.15 a.m. to 1.30 p.m. There is a break of half an hour, 11—11.30 for a light lunch and parents are requested to allow pupils to have this lunch at the school.

"Prep." classes are from 1.30—2.30 p.m. from Monday to Thursday inclusive and all pupils are required to attend them.

Appendix 1d

A FORM ROOM IN THE UPPER SCHOOL.

Uniforms

DRESS. All girls are required to wear white middy blouses, pleated navy-blue skirts, white or navy-blue anklets and black leather shoes. A white dress and a pair of white anklets should be kept for school functions. Each girl should have a pair of white rubber soled for games and drill. High heels and trinkets are forbidden.

HATS & TIES. Until School ties and hatbands are available, navy-blue tie and Stephanos hat with a navy-blue band should be worn.

Hats should be marked inside the crown with each pupil's initials for easy identification.

The teachers will not hold themselves responsible for the loss of pens, jewelry and other articles brought to school by children.

Appendix 1e

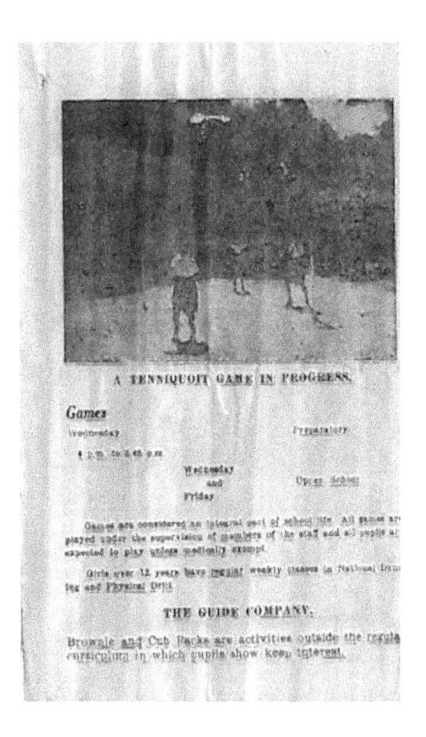

A TENNIQUOIT GAME IN PROGRESS.

Games

Wednesday   Preparatory
4 p.m. to 5.45 p.m.
                    Wednesday
                        and   Upper School
                    Friday

Games are considered an integral part of school life. All games are played under the supervision of members of the staff and all pupils are expected to play unless medically exempt.

Girls over 12 years have regular weekly classes in National Dancing and Physical Drill.

THE GUIDE COMPANY.

Brownie and Cub Packs are activities outside the regular curriculum in which pupils show keen interest.

Appendix 1f

The House System

To foster a spirit of keenness and healthy competition among the children, they are divided into three Houses, viz.:—

AGGREY   PICKENS   BOOKER T. WASHINGTON

Inter-House Competition in all games and athletic activities as well as in work give the children added interest in their school life and training in "team spirit."

Library

The School has a small library, which has been built up mainly through the efforts of the staff and pupils. Contributions of books from parents will be highly appreciated. Graduates of Cameerdown have the privilege of donating a book to the school library on leaving school.

Girls of the Upper School at National Dance.

Appendix 1g

NATIONAL DANCING.

THE QUIET HOUR

On Tuesday mornings at 7.30 pupils who are interested assemble for an hour of meditation and devotion. This is wholly voluntary.

THE COUNSEL CORNER

There is a weekly meeting for adolescents at which difficult problems are discussed and frankly clarified.

THE PARENT-TEACHER'S ASSOCIATION

In 1943 our Parent-Teacher's Association was inaugurated. The object of this was to enable the two vital influences responsible for the building of our children's character to work in co-operation.

Appendix 2

CAMPERDOWN HIGH SCHOOL
Preparatory Department for Boys & Girls
High School for Girls Only.
161 Portland Road, Kingston, Jamaica, B.W.I.

FORM: 5
Report for: Easter
Term Ending: April 1, 1949

SUBJECTS	REMARKS	PERCENTAGE
Religious Knowledge		
English Language		
English Literature — Poetry		
Dictation & Spelling		
Latin		
Spanish		
History		
Mathematics		
Arithmetic	Good, shows effort	
Algebra	shows keen interest	
Geometry		
Needlework	Good	
Art		
Drawing		
Music		
Science		
Geography		
Nature Study		
Hygiene with Physiology	Good	
Athletics		
Keep Fit / Games	Very fair, but needs attention	
Form Mistress' Remarks		
Order Marks		
Unprepared Lessons		No. of times Absent:
Conduct		Late:
Headmistress Remarks		Registration Day For Next Term:

Appendix 3

SCHOOL LEAVING CERTIFICATE

This is to Certify that _____

has completed ... years of Academic Work at CAMPERDOWN HIGH SCHOOL and has reached a satisfactory standard in the following subjects :- English Language, English Literature, Bible Knowledge, History, Geography, Biology, Needlework/Dressmaking, Health Science.

Signed: ....
Headmistress

Date: 6th December 1962

Appendix 4

SCHOOL SONG – "FOUNDATION"
By Winston Bell (Camperdown Past Student)

Father, Hallow this our dwelling
Firmly founded, fashioned fair
Vain its strength and vain its splendor
If Thy Spirit comes not there

Hallow, Lord, our hearts to serve Thee
Make us worthy of this place
Brotherhood and friendship faultless
Bind us here in close embrace

Father, bless our lives with beauty
Hand and brain in skill combine
Vain our art and vain our vigour
If we heed not Thy design

Grant us, Lord, the crown of courage
Strength to strive, till discord cease
Dedicate this school to manhood
Us, Thy ministers of peace

Appendix 5

THE SCHOOL'S GRADUATION SONG
By Winston Bell (Camperdown Past Student)

Step by step
We are leaving school
Oh, what a sad thing
It is for us

Leaving School
It burns me deep down
Oh, we regret this day

Happy days
Oh, happy days we had
Those days of sports and laughter

Leaving school
Leaving happiness
Oh, what a sad thing
It is for us

Teachers and friends we'll miss
What will life be without them?
As we go into the world
Memories will flow forever

CAMPERDOWN, Oh Camperdown
we'll miss you
Oh, how we'll miss sweet Camperdown

Step by step
We are leaving school
Oh, what a sad thing
It is for us

Leaving school
It burns me deep down
Oh, we regret this day

CAMPERDOWN, CAMPERDOWN
CAMPERDOWN, we'll miss you!

Appendix 6

CAMPERDOWN AT THE PENN RELAYS

Hosted annually since 1895 by the University of Pennsylvania at Franklin Field in Philadelphia, the Penn Relays is the oldest and largest track and field competition in the United States. The focus is almost entirely on the running of relay races. The Penn Relays is now an integral part of the Jamaican high schools' track and field calendar.

Girls Winning Team – Championship of America

4x100 metres relay

1989 – 45.13 (R)* (Marie Taylor, Helena Rochester, Revolie Campbell, Andria Lloyd)

1990 – 45.25 (Marie Taylor, Revolie Campbell, Vinette Phillips, Maxine Dawkins)

1992 – 45.37 (Althea Green, Maxine Dawkins, Bridgette Edwards, Marlene Dawkins)

*Note: The record lasted for 9 years (1989-1998)

The 1989 team was inducted to the Penn Relays Wall of Fame in 1997, the second Jamaican girls' high school to win this honour.

Boys Winning Team – Championship of America

4x100 metres relay

1980 – 41.34s (R)* (Howard Lawrence, Wayne Morrison, Oswald Cole, Leroy Reid)

1981 – 40.90s (R)* (Howard Lawrence, Wayne Morrison, Oswald Cole, Leroy Reid)

1983 – 41.42s   (Fitzroy Stephenson, Raymond Stewart, Hugh Fyffe, Shane Howell)

1986 – 40.40s (R)* (Derrick Thomas, Carey Johnson, Ralston Wright, Garfield Campbell)

1987 – 40.99s   (Michael Anderson, Carey Johnson, Ralston Wright, Garfield Campbell)

1989 – 41.23s   (Leon Forrest, Raphael Brown, Trevor Gilbert, Anthony Pryce)

1998 – 40.64s   (Alix Rodriques, David Spencer, Damion Davis, David Lloyd)

2006 – 40.13s (R)* (Kimour Bruce, Remaldo Rose, Rasheed Dwyer, Jermaine Dawkins)

2022 – 40.13s   (Rimando Thomas, Junior Harris, Jason Lewis, Roshawn Clarke)

*Note: Camperdown held the record for this event on four separate occasions. With its 2022 victory in this event, Camperdown is now ranked the top Jamaican high school and is internationally ranked among the winningest high schools in this event.

The 1986 team was inducted to the Penn Relays Wall of Fame in 2003, the first Jamaican boys' high school to win this honour.

Andrew Smith and Leroy Reid were inducted to the Penn Relays Wall of Fame in 2001 as members of the 1986 Texas Christian University 4x200m team.

Carey Johnson and Ralston Wright were also inducted to the Penn Relays Wall of Fame in 2008 as members of the 1991 Texas Christian University 4x100m team, the first collegiate team to run the 4x100m under 39 seconds.

4x400 metres

1985 – 3:11.49s (R) (Michael Warren, Fitzroy Stephenson, Carey Johnson, Alexander Strachan)

2006 – 3:11.46s   (Sandor Pennicot, Remaldo Rose, Rasheed Dwyer, Rayon Lawrence)

                    (Alternates—Dwain Bryden, Saibel Anderson)

Appendix 7a

NATION BUILDERS—FOOTBALL

Camperdown first entered the Manning Cup football competition in 1964. The Manning Cup was donated by Sir William Henry Manning, Governor of Jamaica, for competition among high schools' in the corporate area. The competition first started in 1914.

Camperdown won the Manning Cup in 1978, 1979, and 1982.

The winner of the Manning Cup also competes against the winner of the DaCosta Cup (played for among rural schools) for the Olivier Shield. The Olivier Shield was donated in 1909 by Sir Sydney Olivier, Governor of Jamaica.

Camperdown won the Olivier Shield in 1978 (shared with Clarendon College), 1979, and 1982.

Camperdown won the Walker Cup (played for among the top teams in the Manning Cup) in 1982 and 1988. The Walker Cup is named for Mr. H. N. Walker, Headmaster of Wolmer's Boys School, in recognition of his outstanding years of service to the Inter-Secondary Schools Sports Association.

Many Camperdown players have represented Jamaica at the national senior and junior levels. The following Camperdownians have represented Jamaica at the senior level:

1. Hugh "UU" Bailey
2. Errol "Scarlet Pimpernel" Blake
3. David Burgess
4. Peter "Jair" Cargill
5. *Errol "Clarkie" Clarke
6. Donald "Sammy D" Davidson
7. Ricardo Fuller
8. **Barrington "Cobra" Gaynor

9. **Andrew "Bowa" Hines
10. **Delroy "Zadie Fox" Lewis
11. **Damian Lowe
12. **Thomas McLean
13. **Paul Pringle
14. Kevin Shaw
15. **Ryan "Gadda" Thompson
16. Jamoi Topey
17. Carlton "Spiderman" Williams

* Errol Clarke was the first Camperdown player to be selected on the Jamaica senior team.
** McLean, Lewis, Hines, Gaynor, Thompson, Lowe, and Pringle played in the U.S. on football scholarships.

Appendix 7b

NATION BUILDERS—OLYMPIANS

Donald Quarrie	1968 (Mexico City)
	1972 (Munich)
	1976 (Montreal) Gold – 200m; Silver – 100m
	1980 (Moscow) Bronze – 200m
	1984 (Los Angeles) Silver – 4x100m Relay (Men)
Godfrey Murray	1972
Leroy Reid	1984
Raymond Stewart	1984: Silver – 4x100m Relay (Men)
	1988 (Seoul)
	1992 (Barcelona)
	1996 (Atlanta)
Alex Stewart (Boxing)	1984
Andrew Smith	1988
Laurel Johnson	1988
Ralston Wright	1992
Andria Lloyd	1996: Bronze – 4x100m Relay (Women)
Ronetta Smith	2004 (Athens) Bronze – 4x400m Relay (Women)
Rasheed Dwyer	2020 (2021) (Tokyo)
Britany Anderson	2020 (2021)

Appendix 8

THE C'DOWN 100: CHANGEMAKERS

Profiles of 100 of Camperdown's accomplished graduates, who symbolize excellence in various realms, building the Camperdown brand and establishing a legacy for others to follow. They have been recognized over the years for personal achievements and noble qualities in uplifting the profile of the school and the country, nationally and internationally.

1. Anderson, Rosemarie – Teacher (Physical Education, Geography), Camperdown High School. Transportation Engineer, United States Department of Transportation; United States Federal Highway System; Traffic Engineer for Operations, JFK Airport, New York.
2. Anderson, Dr. Viola – Medical Doctor (Internal Medicine), New York and Houston, Texas.
3. Anthony, Carol (Legister) – Superintendent, Maxfield Park Children's Home, Jamaica.
4. Ashley, Sylvia (Henry) – Director, International Affairs and Fundraising, Andrew Young Foundation, Atlanta, Georgia; President, Jamaica Secretaries Association.
5. Bailey, Valentine – Principal, Camperdown High School (2010 –)
6. Bell, Winston – Pastor, Businessman, Songwriter. One of the most prominent actors in Jamaica's entertainment industry, part of legendary comedy team "Bello and Blacka." Writer of Camperdown's school song, "Foundation," and graduation song, "Leaving School." Camperdown Hall of Fame (2016).
7. Blackford, Richard – Artist.
8. Brooks, Sandra (Llewellyn) – Evangelist; Lead singer of international gospel group, The Grace Thrillers. Recipient of Jamaica Federation of Musicians "Award of Excellence" (1998).
9. Brown, Waldo – Teacher (Physics and Mathematics), Camperdown High School and Camperdown Extension School; Insurance

Executive. President, Camperdown Past Students Association, New York. Camperdown Hall of Fame (2018).
10. Bryan, Ambassador Dr. Basil K. – Diplomat; Academic; Author; Professor. Consul General of Jamaica in New York (1998-2007). Consultant, Government of Jamaica. Recognized by New York *Carib News* as one of "100 most Outstanding Jamaican Achievers in the United States" (2021). Recipient of Order of Distinction (O.D.) (2002). Recipient of two United States Congressional Awards (2005, 2007). Recipient of Jamaica's Musgrave Medal (Bronze) (2017). Camperdown Hall of Fame (2012).
11. Bryan, Jean M. (Pinnock) – University Administrator; Educator, Counselor and Advisor; Director, College of Arts and Sciences, Howard University, Washington, D.C.
12. Campbell, Joyce – Director, Consumer Education, Ministry of Industry and Commerce, Jamaica.
13. Cargill, Peter – Professional footballer and Coach. One of best footballers (and most capped) to represent Jamaica; described as "midfield general" and "authoritative leader." Vice-Captain of Jamaica national football team (World Cup finals, 1998). Camperdown Hall of Fame (2012).
14. Chambers, Trevor – Officer, Jamaica Constabulary Force. Associate Director of Security, St. Thomas University, Florida.
15. Clarke, Sonia (Jones) – Administrative Assistant, New York. President, Camperdown Past Students Association, N.Y.
16. Cooke, Cynthia P. (Warren) – Principal, Camperdown High School (1993-2010). Author; Treasurer, ISSA; General Secretary— Racers Track Club; Co-Founder of the Camperdown Classics track meet. Justice of the Peace. Order of Distinction (O.D.) (2015). Camperdown Hall of Fame (2014).
17. Cooper, Michelle (Chue Sang) – Director of Procurement, City University of New York; Senior Contract Officer, Columbia University, New York. President, Camperdown Past Students Association of South Florida. Recipient of Ivy Grant Award of Excellence (2012).
18. Cunningham, Dr. Allan – Lecturer; Global Jamaica Diaspora Council representative for Southern United States. Founder, "People

Profile," Florida. President, Camperdown Past Students Association of South Florida.
19. DaCosta, Alfred "Teddy" – Businessman/Entrepreneur. Signart Printing; Labels and Supplies Centre, Jamaica.
20. Davis, Opal – Community builder and volunteer; Justice of the Peace; Badge of Honour for Meritorious Service (2017). Recipient of Ivy Grant Award for Outstanding Service (2019).
21. DeCambre, Emmett – Social Worker; Supervisor, Deputy Director, A P Services, New York.
22. Dewdney, Dr. Trevor – (Camperdown Prep)—Veterinary Surgeon; Chairman, RADA Advisory Committee; Director, National Development Bank; Jamaica Broilers Group; Agricultural Development Corporation; Order of Distinction (O.D.) (1998).
23. Dixon, Anthony – Businessman/Entrepreneur – ADD Enterprises. Recipient of Ivy Grant Award for Distinguished Service (2015).
24. Drummond, Anthony – Officer, Jamaica Constabulary Force. Security Supervisor, New York.
25. Dwyer, Rasheed – International Athlete; Olympian (2020); 3-time national champion in 200m; Commonwealth Games Gold medal in 200m (2014); Gold medal—4x100m relay – World Relays (2014); Gold Medal—4x100m relay—World Athletics Championships (2015).
26. Forrester, Claire – Journalist, Author, Sportswriter. Secretary—Press Association of Jamaica. Founding member/General Secretary, Association of Caribbean Media Workers. Life member—Press Association of Jamaica. Exceptional Leadership Award from Pan American Health Organization (2006). Order of Distinction (O.D.) (2013). Camperdown Hall of Fame (2016).
27. Franklin, Maxine – International Classical Concert Pianist.
28. Fuller, Ricardo – Professional footballer (English Premier League). One of most gifted footballers to come from Jamaica.
29. Garvey, Dr. Julius – (Camperdown Prep)—Cardiac-Thoracic Surgeon. Fellow, Royal College of Surgeons; Fellow, American College of Surgeons. President – Universal Negro Improvement Association/African Communities League. Order of Jamaica (2019).
30. Garwood, Anthony – International Referee (FIFA). Vice-Principal of

Camperdown High School; Principal, Charlie Smith High School; Principal, Dinthill Technical High School.
31. Grant, Heather – Jamaica Festival Song winner (1992).
32. Golding, Annie – National representative in Track and Field. National Representative (Captain) in Softball. Holder of West Indies record in Discus (1960).
33. Gordon, Dennis – Businessman; Politician. Chairman, Jacden Enterprise Ltd.; Councillor, Kingston and St. Andrew Municipal Corporation. President, Camperdown Past Students Association, Jamaica.
34. Gordon Martin, Andrea (Evering) – Assistant General Manager, JN General Insurance Company Ltd, Jamaica.
35. Harris, Dr. Marcianne (Harriott) – Educator; Professor. Board of Education, New York. College of New Rochelle, New York; Iona University, New York.
36. Heslop, Donna – Businesswoman/Entrepreneur; Real Estate Professional, Maryland.
37. Hibbert, Peter – Businessman; Pastor. President, Waterhouse Football Club; Manager, Jamaica U-23 Football team; National representative in Pistol Shooting.
38. Hinds, Wavell – Professional cricketer in England and India. West Indies test cricketer; Captain – Jamaica cricket team; President, West Indies Players Association. President, Camperdown Past Students Association, Jamaica. Camperdown Hall of Fame (2013).
39. Hobson, Dr. Winston – Attorney at Law; Agricultural Scientist; Lecturer. Asst. Public Defender, Des Moines, Iowa. Asst. Public Defender, Miami-Dade County, Fla. Camperdown Hall of Fame (2018).
40. James, Icilda (Allen) – Advisor – Customer Service, Jamaica Telephone Company; Jamaica Diaspora Group, Zimbabwe.
41. Johnson, Laurel – Olympian (1988); Sports Massage Therapist/Chiropractor, Florida..
42. Lewis, Hopeton – Singer and Songwriter; Businessman. His song, "Take It Easy," considered as the originator of the Rock Steady beat. Jamaica Festival Song winner (1970). In 2012 was named among 50 entertainers lauded for contribution to Jamaican music. Camperdown Hall of Fame (2013).

43. Lindsay, Delroy – Banker; Businessman; News Commentator.
44. Lindsay, Louis – Lecturer, Author, Public Servant. Research Fellow, Institute of Social and Economic Research, University of the West Indies. Consultant, Government of Jamaica; Chief Technical Director, Ministry of Parliamentary and Regional Affairs; Permanent Secretary, Ministry of Local Government and Community Development. Chairman, Office of Disaster Preparedness.
45. Linton, Dr. Hazel (Camperdown Extension) – Education and Mental Health, Hartford, Connecticut.
46. Livingston, Neville O'Riley (Bunny Wailer) – Singer/Songwriter; Founding member of world-famous Wailers Band (with Bob Marley and Peter Tosh). Three-time winner of Grammy Award. Order of Distinction (CD) (1996); Order of Jamaica (2012); Order of Merit (2017). Camperdown Hall of Fame (2011).
47. Lloyd, Andria – Olympian (1996). Winner of bronze medal – (4x100m) at 1996 Olympic Games in Atlanta, U.S.A.
48. Lowe, Damion – Professional footballer. Captain—Jamaica national football team, the "Reggae Boyz."
49. Lucie-Smith, Jackie – Public Servant; Permanent Secretary (Acting), Ministry of Education. Jamaica Female Invitational Touring Hockey team. Order of Distinction (2006).
50. Maylor, Dr. Daphne Hortense (Ruddock) – Medical Doctor (Pediatrics), New York.
51. McFarlane, Lt. Commander John – Jamaica Coast Guard; Concert Soloist/Multi-Instrumentalist; Custos of St. Andrew (Acting); Order of Distinction (O.D.) (2015).
52. McKenzie, Norman – Chemist; Researcher – Scientific Research Council, Jamaica. Director of Credit, Florida.
53. McKnight, Franklin – Journalist and Lecturer. Associate Editor, **The Daily Gleaner**. Managing Editor, Jamaica Herald newspaper; founder North Coast Times. Order of Distinction (O.D.) (2014). Camperdown Hall of Fame (2019).
54. McLean, Adrian – Pastor; Teacher (Sociology, Ethics, Religious Education), Camperdown High School.
55. Mills Glen – One of the most famous Track and Field coaches in the world; guided Usain Bolt to world records in 100m, 200m,

and 4x100m relay. Over 3 decades as coach of Camperdown's famous "sprint factory" track team. Coach of Jamaica's national track teams for 22 years. Meet Director – ISSA Champs for 25+ years. Founder/President/Head Coach of Racers Track Club. Co-founder Camperdown Classics track meet. Order of Distinction (O.D.) (2002); Order of Distinction (C.D.) (2008); Order of Jamaica (O.J.) (2014). Recipient of Doctor of Laws (LL.D.) from University of the West Indies (2012). IAAF Lifetime Achievement Award (2012). Camperdown Hall of Fame (2011).

56. Mitchell, Victoria (Stephenson) – Executive Director, AFSCME Union, N.Y.
57. Montieth, Beverly (Welsh) – President, Jamaica Nurses Association of Florida.
58. Murray, Dr. Barrington – Medical Doctor (Obstetrics and Gynecology), Florida. Camperdown Hall of Fame (2014).
59. Murray, Godfrey – Olympian (1972). Businessman, Physical Therapist, Florida.
60. Nelson, Dr. Joyce (Brown) – Mathematician; Lecturer.
61. Orridge, Camille – Social Change Agent; Chief Executive Officer, Toronto Central Local Health Integration Network. Canada's "Women of Influence" award (2012); Canada's "Excellence in Medicine" award (2014).
62. Owen, Valerie (Johnson) – Senior Financial Associate, N.Y.U. Langone Health, New York; President, Camperdown Past Students Association, New York.
63. Payne, Patrick – Businessman; Lecturer. Founder, All-Island Games, New York. Founding President, Camperdown Past Students Association, New York.
64. Peralto, Ryan – (Camperdown Prep) – Member of Parliament; Minister of State; Mayor, City of Kingston, Jamaica.
65. Phillips, Venesha – Attorney at Law, Politician; Councillor, Kingston and St. Andrew Municipal Corporation.
66. Powell, Judge Jackie – Broward County Court, 17th Judicial Circuit of Florida. Camperdown Hall of Fame – (2019).
67. Potopsingh, Dr. Ruth (Williams) – Teacher (Geography), Camperdown High School; Development Planner/Environmentalist.

Group Managing Director, Petroleum Corporation of Jamaica. Head, Caribbean Sustainable Energy and Innovation Institute, University of Technology, Jamaica.

68. Quarrie, Donald O'Riley – 5-time Olympian (1968, 1972, 1976, 1980, 1984); winner of Olympic Gold, Silver and Bronze medals. First Jamaican to win a sprint title at Olympic Games. Only sprinter to simultaneously hold world record in 100y and 100m. Named by Track and Field magazine as top 200m runner in the 1970s. 5-time Jamaica Sportsman of the Year; Order of Distinction (O.D.) (1975); Order of Distinction (C.D.) (2008). California Sports Hall of Fame (2008). Coach and Manager of Jamaica's teams to Olympic Games and International meets. Camperdown Hall of Fame (2011).

69. Reid, Carole – One of Jamaica's most admired and awarded Sopranos. Lead singer at numerous national events, including State functions. Represented Jamaica at 35th International Eisteddfod. Recipient of Jamaica's Musgrave Medal (Bronze) (1999); Governor General's Achievement Award (2012).

70. Rennalls, Sylvia (Anderson-Manning) – Administrator, Webster Memorial United Church. Manager, Royal Bank of Jamaica, Ltd.

71. Richards, Robin – Lieutenant II, Detective Commanding Officer; Operations, South Bureau Vice and Human Trafficking Coordinator; Cost Accountant, Los Angeles, California.

72. Ricketts, Patsy – Principal dancer of the National Dance Theatre Company (NDTC) of Jamaica. Founding member of Harlem Dance Company. Recipient of National Badge of Honour for Service to Education (2008). Camperdown Hall of Fame (2011).

73. Rogers, Hazelle (Bax) – Mayor of City of Lauderdale Lakes, Florida. First Jamaican elected to Florida House of Representatives. Order of Distinction (O.D.) (2020).

74. Rowe, Devon – Financial Secretary of Jamaica. Chairman PetroCaribe Fund; Chairman Capital Development Fund; Director Bank of Jamaica. Recipient of Order of Distinction (C.D.) – (2014). Camperdown Hall of Fame (2013).

75. Ruddock, Dr. Peter – Scientist; Lecturer; Author. President, Camperdown Past Students Association (Jamaica); Member, Camperdown High School Board of Governors; President, Jamaica

High School Alumni Association. Manager, Petroleum Corporation of Jamaica.
76. Scarlett, Brenda (Robinson) – Nursing Administrator/Social Worker, University Hospital of the West Indies. "Nurse of the Year" (1996).
77. Simpson, Faith – Administrative Assistant, Florida. Founding President, Camperdown Past Students Association, Florida.
78. Smith, Dr. Alva – Medical Doctor (Cardiologist, specialist in Cardiovascular diseases). Chief of Medicine and Director, Pennsylvania. Camperdown Hall of Fame (2013).
79. Smith, Andrew – Olympian (1988); winner of Bronze medal in 4x100m relay, World Athletics Championships in 1987.
80. Smith, June – Entrepreneur; Founder/CEO, TAJJ Cosmetics, Canada; International Innovator of Color Award (U.K.), 2018.
81. Smith, Ronetta – Olympian (2004). Winner of Olympic medal (Bronze) as member of Jamaica's 4x400m relay team in Olympic Games in Athens, Greece in 2004.
82. Smith, Winifred (Crooks) – Principal, Camperdown High School (1983-1993). Treasurer, ISSA. Order of Distinction (O.D.) (1992). Camperdown Hall of Fame (2013).
83. Stewart, Raymond Douglas – 4-time Olympian (1984, 1988, 1992, 1996). First Jamaican to break 10-second barrier in the 100 meters. First sprinter in history to make 3 successive Olympics 100m finals. Camperdown Hall of Fame (2012).
84. Strachan, Grace – Director, Human Resources Development Dept., United Nations; International Labor Organization, Geneva, Switzerland. Director, Planning Institute of Jamaica.
85. Stubbs-Ruddock, Jefferine – Attorney at Law; Prosecutor (Resident Magistrate Court); Senior Legal Officer, National Land Agency; Legal Counsel, National Housing Trust, Jamaica.
86. Taffe, Hugh – Banking Administrator, New York.
87. Taylor, Ambassador Marjorie – Public Servant. Councillor, Kingston and St. Andrew Municipal Corporation; Senator; Member of Parliament for Constituency of East Kingston and Port Royal; Minister of State; Ambassador for Children Services.
88. Thomas, Dr. Robert – Veterinarian.
89. Thomas, Victor – Track Coach, Lincoln University of Missouri.

90. Valentine, Dr. Muriel (Lowe) – (Camperdown Prep)—One of 10 women in inaugural class in 1948 to study medicine at University College of the West Indies. Leading expert in the Caribbean in Sarcoidosis. Registrar of Medical Council of Jamaica (2008-2011). Recipient of Order of Distinction (C.D.) (1986); Order of Jamaica (O.J.) (2009. Camperdown Hall of Fame (2012).

91. Walter, Irene (Reid) – Educator. Pro-Chancellor, International University of the Caribbean. Assistant Registrar, University of the West Indies; Registrar, Norman Manley Law School; Registrar, Caribbean Examination Council. Recipient of Order of Distinction (CD) (1998). Distinguished Graduate Award, UWI (1998). Vice-Chair, Camperdown High School Board of Governors; Camperdown Hall of Fame (2012).

92. Warren, Dr. Stanilaus – Lecturer; Consultant (Medical and Sports Sociology).

93. Watson, William – Businessman; Company Director, ADLIB Studio, Jamaica. President, Camperdown Past Students Association, Jamaica.

94. Waugh, Patricia (Reid) – Teacher (Mathematics), Calabar High School; Chartered Accountant, St. Maarten; Regulator, Financial Services, Nevis.

95. Wiley, Sandra (Pinnock) – Nursing Administrator; Supervisor – Pediatric Intensive Care Unit, Children's Hospital, Florida.

96. Williams, Derrick – International Dancer; Alvin Ailey Dance Company, New York.

97. Williams, Kenneth – Program Manager Specialist with United States Agency for International Development (USAID). Teacher (Accounting), Camperdown High School. Recipient of Ivy Grant Award for Outstanding Contributions to Camperdown High School (2016).

98. Williams, Ralph – Vice-Principal, Camperdown High School; Principal, Charlemont High School.

99. Wint, Rainford – Sales Executive, The Gleaner Company.

100. Young, Desmond – Singer/Musician. Festival Song finalist, 1973. President, Jamaica Federation of Musicians; Founding Director—Jamaica Association of Composers, Authors and Publishers.

Sources

In addition to numerous personal interviews, biographies, obituaries, booklets, magazines, etc., other sources utilized included the following:

Camperdown High School 60th Anniversary magazine (1930 – 1990)
Camperdown High School (Flame magazine – various issues).
Carifta Games records, 1972-2005.
Handbook of Jamaica (various years)
JP Publications Limited. *A Complete Record of Jamaica in World Athletics, 1930-1987*. (Undated) Kingston, Jamaica.
Lawrence, Hubert, et al. *"Champs 100" – A Century of Jamaican High School Athletics: 1910-2010*. Great House OmniMedia Ltd., Kingston, Jamaica (2010).
Miller, Errol. *Jamaican Society and High Schooling*. Institute of Social and Economic Research, University of the West Indies, 1990.
Penn Relays (Carnival) programmes (Various years).
SportsLife Magazine
Sports Annual Magazine
Synod Papers (annual) – United Church of Jamaica and Grand Cayman (various years)
The Daily Gleaner (1930-2010)

INDEX

All Manning, 58, 68, 70–71, 74, 77, 81-82, 91-92, 99
All Schools, 29, 43, 62, 75, 82, 140
Anderson, Lois (Stewart), 44-45, 121
Anderson, Roland, 57, 64, 70
Anderson, Rosemarie, 73-75, 190
Anderson, Sylvia, 52, 54, 134, 196
Anderson, Viola, 115, 138-39, 190
Aquart, Lennox "Bobby", 45, 49, 57, 58, 59, 61, 111
Archer, Roy, 29, 56, 139
Assassin (Jeffrey Campbell), 125
Attride, Anthony, 59, 61, 62, 87, 140

Baby Cham (Damian Beckett), 125
Bailey, Hugh, 75-77, 187
Bailey, Valentine, *i*, *ix*, 90, 119, 124, 190
Barrett, Eric, *iv*, 71–73, 87, 143
Basketball, 53, 64, 103, 104, 108, 119, 156
Bell, Winston, 76, 97, 116, 181, 183, 190
Blake, Errol, 80–82, 148-49, 161, 187
Bolt, Usain, 80, 118, 126, 194
Brown, Jeff, *ix*, 65, 71, 75, 87-89, 114, 122, 124, 147-48, 150, 161
Brown, Winston "Danny", 71-73
Bryan, Basil, 46, 49, 52, 54, 57, 59, 116, 126, 142, 154, 191
Bryan, Christeina, 119
Bryan, Jean Pinnock, *Dedication*, *vi*, 6, 50, 52, 56, 111, 131, 137, 142, 154, 191
Burgess, David, 75, 77, 187
Burke, Myrtle, 4, 26, 27, 47, 137
Burrowes, Sydney "Foggy", 58, 61, 94
Buxton High School, 15, 28, 29, 65

Campbell, Garfield, 92, 93, 97, 187

Campbell, Revolie, 69, 93–95, 185
Camperdown Classics, 118, 153, 191, 195
Camperdown Girl School, *xiii*, 17, 20, 21, 24, 53
Camperdown School, 17, 22, 29, 33, 34
Cargill, Peter, 82, 91, 105, 126, 149, 151, 161, 187, 191
Carifta Games, 74, 76, 77, 80, 81, 86-88, 92-95, 97, 100, 101, 104, 117-18, 199
CASI—Camperdown Association of Social Intervention, 96, 120,
Cheerleading, 117
Chess, 80, 83, 105, 116
Coke, Reverend Raymond, 75
Comet Relays, 94
Commonwealth Games, 70, 76, 117, 192
Cooke, Cynthia, *iv*, *ix*, 7, 96, 100-102, 112, 113, 118–20, 124, 153, 191
Cooper, Michelle Chue Sang, 122, 191
Crawford, Lloyd, 80, 82-83, 148-49, 161
Cricket, 44, 46, 49, 56, 64, 66, 70, 76, 78, 80, 82, 95
Crooks, Winifred, 6, 9, 25, 46, 88-89, 197; *see also* Smith, Winifred
Cunningham, Alan, 90, 122, 191

Dawkins, Marlene, 94, 95, 100, 101, 112, 185
Dawkins, Maxine, 94, 95, 100, 101, 112, 185
DeCambre, Emmett, *iv*, 77, 80, 192
Dixon, Dennis, 52, 57, 58, 67, 68, 141
Donalds, Gladstone, 46, 109
Drama Festival, 52, 54, 56, 63, 69, 70, 73, 76, 79, 81, 85, 96, 97, 105, 120
Dwyer, Rasheed, 117, 118, 125, 153, 154, 156, 189, 192
Dunoon Park, 57

Edman, Willard, 48, 52, 57
Excelsior School, 9, 11, 15, 19, 25, 28, 49, 58, 62, 64, 67, 82, 85, 88, 101
Extension School, 42, 43, 56, 58, 63, 65, 71, 72, 74, 77-79, 145, 190

Facey, Llewellyn, 56–59, 61-62, 140
Fitz-Gordon, Rodney, 68-69, 87
Fletcher, Everald, *iv*, 43, 52, 157
Forbes, Raphael, 47, 52, 65, 113, 121, 133, 142
Forrester, Claire, 50, 122, 192
Fuller, Ricardo, 104, 126, 187, 192

Garvey, Amy Jacques, 19
Gibson Relays, 74, 85-86, 95
Glasspole, Florizel, 9, 22, 29, 40
Glasspole House, 29
The Gleaner, v, 17-19, 21-22, 53, 59, 67, 77, 82, 94, 108, 141, 147, 149, 155, 194, 198-99
Golding, Annie, 29-30, 39
Gordon, Dennis, 80, 122, 147, 193
Graham, Raymond "KC", 95, 152
Grant, Ivy May, *ii-vii, xiv*, 1, 4-11, 16-37, 40, 45; *see also* Wilson, Ivy May
Grant House, 29

Harriott, Oscar, 2, 9, 24, 43, 46
Harris, Marcianne Harriott, *iv*, 13, 26, 28, 193
Hewitt, Althea, 97, 125
Hibbert, Peter, 76-77, 82, 87, 149, 161, 193
Hinds, Wavell, 103, 126, 193
Hobson, Winston, 57, 67-68, 142, 193
Home School, *xiii*, 3, 14, 17, 20

Johnson, Carey, 69, 93, 97, 186

Kellier, Myrtle, *ix*, 86, 89, 113
Kensington Park, 20, 57, 59, 82, 133, 147
King, Keith, 46, 57, 59, 136
Kingston College, 15, 21, 43, 47

Lewis, Hopeton, 64, 125, 193
Lindsay, Louis, 52, 54, 66, 126, 194
Livingston, Neville (Bunny Wailer), 111, 125, 158, 194
Llewellyn, Audrey, 69, 77, 80-81, 86, 112
Llewellyn, Sandra, 97, 190
Lloyd, Andria 69, 93–95, 152, 185, 189, 194
Lucas Cricket Club, 18, 21

Malcolm, Nora, 4, 5, 11, 26, 27, 37

Manley, Norman, 12, 41-42
Manning Cup, 57, 58, 61–68, 73, 75, 80–85, 91-92, 99, 103, 114, 148, 161, 187
Mayne, Diane, 86, 113, 116
Maynard, Eric, 80, 82, 148-149, 161
McFarlane, Ruby, 26, 47, 54, 63
McKenzie, Norman, 49, 52, 54, 194
McLean, Adrian, *iv*, 109, 112, 194
McLean, Thomas, 74, 80-81, 147-48, 188
McLeod, William, 90, 96, 107
McPherson, Isobel, 4, 26, 27, 134
Meeks, Merle Wilson, *iv*, 19, 24,
Melbourne, Earl, 76, 77, 80, 147
Merl Grove High School, 15, 19, 20, 28, 55, 88
Messam, Henry McD, 23, 29, 41, 57, 59-60, 62, 67-68, 142
Miller, Douglas, 27-30, 41-42, 51, 98, 109, 131-32
Miller House, 28-29
Mills, Glen, *iv*, 60, 68-69, 72 –74, 87, 112, 118, 143, 194
Mills House, 118
Minzie, Patrick, 64, 68, 71-72, 142-43
Mission Possible, 109, 115
Moffat, Sharon, 69, 75–77, 81,
Murray, Barrington, 114, 195
Murray, Godfrey, 62, 64, 67–69, 87, 141-42, 189, 195
Murray, Michael, 57, 59, 61-62, 87, 139-40

Netball, 23, 44, 46, 49, 66, 70-71, 73-74, 99, 103, 119, 150, 160

Olivier, Shield, 66, 82, 84, 91, 149, 161, 187
Olympics, 48, 68, 76, 93, 112, 118, 124-25, 146, 197
Operation English, 89, 98

Panton, Pearline, 44, 46, 56
Past Students Association, *iii*, 18, 53, 56, 70, 76, 91, 121-22, 191–198
Penn Relays, 62, 68-69, 71, 85–87, 90, 93, 95-98, 101, 103, 117-18, 126, 140-43, 150, 154, 185-86, 199

Phillips, Vinette, 94-95, 185
Pinnock, Carol, 52, 111, 139
Pinnock-Wiley, Sandra, v, 50, 111, 135-37
Presbyterian Church, 6, 22, 27-28, 30-31, 36, 40, 46, 50-51, 54, 56, 70

Quarrie, Donald, 59, 61–64, 67–69, 70, 76-77, 80, 85, 87, 93, 111, 124, 140–142, 146, 153, 189, 196
Quarrie, Edward, 68, 71, 87, 111, 143
Quarrie House, 85

Reform of Secondary Education, 107
Reid, Carole, 11, 153
Reid, Leroy, 85–87, 124, 150, 185-86, 189
Reid, Melvie, 47, 52, 63, 64
Ricketts, Patsy, 72, 116, 196
Rochester, Helena, 95, 185
Rose, Remaldo, 117-18, 154, 186
Ruddock, Peter, 90, 122, 196

Sangster, Ferdinand, 9, 29, 41, 51, 68, 71, 99, 123, 132
Sangster House, 71
Schools Drama Festival, 52, 54, 56, 63, 69-70, 73, 76, 79, 81, 85, 96-97, 105
Seventh-day Adventist, *xiii*, 1, 2, 8-9, 13, 88
Smith, Andrew, 69, 90, 124, 186, 189, 197
Smith, Ethlyn, 29, 50-53
Smith, Ronetta, 69, 125, 189, 197
Smith, Winifred, *iv, ix,* 6, 9, 30, 46, 79, 86, 88, 101, 121, 124, 142, 197; *see also* Crooks, Winifred
Softball, 28–30, 39, 44, 46, 49-50, 56, 59, 65, 93, 108, 139, 193
Spencer, David, 103-04, 186
Spragga Benz (Carlton Grant), 125
Sprint Factory, *i*, 69, 87, 195
St. Andrew Scots Kirk, 50, 54, 56, 67, 86, 98
Stewart, Raymond, 69, 87-88, 90–93, 124, 186, 189, 197
Strachan, Grace, 55, 70, 197

Taylor, Barrington, 53, 57, 59, 61-62, 111, 140
Taylor, Marie, 93, 95, 185
Taylor, Marjorie, 126, 197
Taffe, Hugh, 64, 67–69, 142, 197
Tappin Cup, 66, 77, 80, 82, 147
Thomas, Mugabe, 104
Tomlinson, Percival, 80, 82, 147

United Church, *v*, 30, 75, 78, 86, 101, 109, 196, 199

Walker Cup, 66, 75, 82, 91-92, 187
Walter, Irene Reid, *iv*, 10, 25, 68, 114, 198
Walters, Jackie, 80, 91-92, 148-49, 161
Watson, William, *iii*, 122, 198
Wayne Wonder (Von Wayne Charles), 125
Webber, Verone, 69, 74, 76-77
West Indies Training College (High School), 1, 2, 9
White, Noel, *ix*, 44-45, 47-49, 131-32
Williams, Carlton, 75, 77, 80-82, 112, 147–149, 161, 188
Williams, Derrick, 48, 54, 116, 198
Williams, Ralph, 89, 104, 113
Williams, Stanley, 79, 86, 113
Wilson, Ivy May, *ii*, 1-4, 9, 12-18, 26; *see also* Grant, Ivy May
Wright, Ralston, 69, 97, 186, 189

Young, Desmond, 125, 158, 198

ONLY THE BEST IS GOOD ENOUGH

"Prayer is the answer to every problem in life. It puts us in tune with divine wisdom which knows how to adjust everything perfectly. So often we do not pray in certain situations, because from our standpoint, the outlook is hopeless. But nothing is impossible with God. Nothing is so entangled that it cannot be remedied; no human relationship is too strained for God to bring about reconciliation and understanding; no habit so deep-rooted that it cannot be overcome; no one is so weak that he cannot be strong; no one is so ill that he cannot be healed. No mind is so dull that it cannot be made brilliant. Whatever we need, if we trust God, He will supply it. If anything is causing worry or anxiety, let us stop rehearsing the difficulty and trust God for healing, love and power."

(Ellen G. White)